D0345966

WYE VALLEY WALKS FOR MOTORISTS

Warne Gerrard Guides for Walkers

Walks for Motorists Series

CHESHIRE WALKS

CHILTERNS WALKS
        Northern
        Southern

COTSWOLDS WALKS
        Northern
        Southern

EXMOOR WALKS

JERSEY WALKS

LAKE DISTRICT WALKS
        Central
        Northern
        Western

LONDON COUNTRYSIDE WALKS
        North West
        North East
        South West
        South East

GREEN LONDON WALKS
        (both circular and cross country)

MIDLAND WALKS

NORTH YORK MOORS WALKS
        North and East
        West and South

PEAK DISTRICT WALKS

PENDLESIDE AND BRONTE COUNTRY WALKS

SNOWDONIA WALKS
        Northern

SOUTH DOWNS WALKS

WYE VALLEY WALKS

YORKSHIRE DALES WALKS

FURTHER DALES WALKS

Long Distance and Cross Country Walks

WALKING THE PENNINE WAY

RAMBLES IN THE DALES

WYE VALLEY

WALKS FOR MOTORISTS

Peter A. Price

30 sketch maps and
4 line drawings by the author
6 photographs by the author

FREDERICK WARNE

Published by
Frederick Warne (Publishers) Ltd
40 Bedford Square
London WC1B 3HE

© 1979

The front cover shows the river Wye from Holme Lacy; the back cover picture is of a foresters' road in Tintern Forest.

Publisher's Note

The length of each walk in this book is given in miles and kilometres, but within the text Imperial Measurements are quoted. It is useful to bear the following approximations in mind: 5 miles = 8 kilometres, $\frac{1}{2}$ mile = 805 metres, 1 metre = 39.4 inches.

ISBN 0 7232 2147 2

Phototypeset by Tradespools Ltd., Frome, Somerset
Printed by Galava Printing Co. Ltd., Nelson, Lancashire

Contents

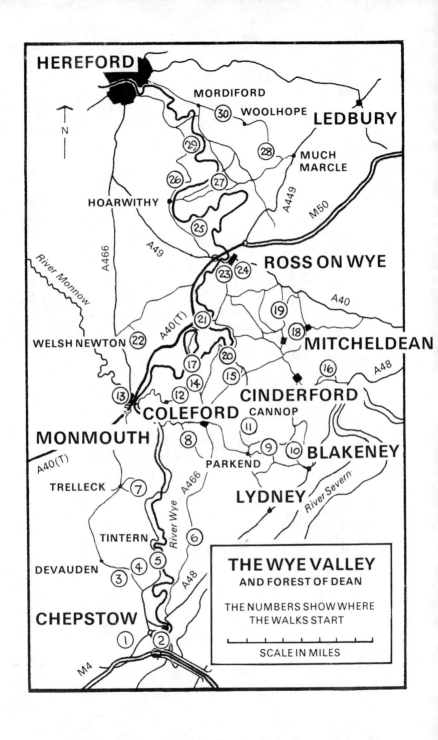

Introduction

The Wye Valley from Hereford to Chepstow is one of the most picturesque regions of Britain. In the northern part the river winds through the lush pastures of south Herefordshire and in the southern part it has cut its way down through 600 feet of rock, so that it now runs in a narrow, tree-covered valley. The whole region has been designated as an Area of Outstanding Natural Beauty.

When the south of Britain was beginning to warm up at the end of the last Ice Age we know that man was living in a cave on the banks of the Wye near Symonds Yat. That was some twelve thousand years ago and man has been in the Wye Valley ever since. Over the years he shaped the countryside to his needs as best he could. Megaliths and mounds, all dating back to the twilight age, are still to be seen, though their purpose is long since forgotten. The presence of eight hilltop earthworks, all within a four mile radius just southeast of Hereford, indicate not only that later raiders were able to penetrate easily up the river Wye but that local settlements must have been quite large. Indeed it is now realised that by the 2nd century BC much of Britain already supported a large settled population.

With the Romans came stability and the development of Dean Iron. This was surface mined wherever the ore outcropped in narrow gullies or 'Scowles' as they are called. In the north of the area there was a slow but constant change, the result of new farming methods. In the south there was an ever-increasing demand for iron and timber and later coal. The intricate pattern of tramways and railways bears testimony to the energy of the iron and coal industries at the height of their prosperity. Today the north continues its gradual change, with machines replacing human labour, but in the south almost all industry has ended, and is being replaced by farming – the farming of trees.

To get the most out of these walks – or any walk – it is necessary to put more in than just walking-power. It is hoped that the observations made along the way will help to make the walks more interesting. Much more could be mentioned, but space will not allow.

All walks in this book are circular. They start and finish at the same place. The routes described are on public rights-of-way as shown on the Definitive Map or the County Road Record or on the Forestry Commission land to which the public have access. 'Members of the Public are permitted to enter Forestry Commission land entirely at their own risk on condition that they will have no claim whatsoever against the Forestry Commission for any loss, damage or injury howsoever suffered or caused'. Some of the walks go through farmland or private woodland which is the source of income to the farmer.

Damage to fences, walls or gates may cause suffering to animals who could get out and eat the wrong food or be injured by a car – apart from the expense involved in repairs.

If you see a fire in the forest put it out if you can – if not, telephone the fire brigade (999).

Make sure you observe the country code:

> Guard against fire risk.
> Fasten all gates.
> Keep dogs under proper control.
> Keep to the paths across farmland.
> Avoid damaging fences, hedges and walls.
> Leave no litter.
> Safeguard water supplies.
> Protect wild life, wild plants and trees.
> Go carefully on country roads.
> Respect the life of the countryside.

The most important item of equipment for the walker is footwear. You may come across quite a lot of mud even in summer so the best protection is to have a lightweight pair of boots. Most walkers get them a size too big and then wear an extra pair of thick socks to stop them rubbing. When turned down over the top of the boot they will stop small stones getting down under the feet. When you get back to the car you can take them off and change back into clean shoes. Boots are also advisable when the ground is hard and dry because the muddy gateways and tracks dry into very uneven ground and it is easy to twist an ankle in an unguarded moment.

The number of the 1/50,000 Ordnance Survey Sheet which covers the area concerned is given at the beginning of each walk. An * indicates that all the walk and (*) that part of the walk is covered by the 1/25,000 Leisure Map: Wye Valley and Forest of Dean. To have a map of the district adds considerable interest to a walk, as it is possible to identify distant objects not shown on the sketch map.

On the Geology of The Dean Region

The walks in the northern area described in this book are mainly over Old Red Sandstone. The exception is in the area around Woolhope where the deeper layers of limestone have been pushed up and are exposed (Walks 28 to 30). The lower Wye Valley and the adjoining Forest of Dean are quite unusual and form one of the centres of pilgrimage for geologists from all over Britain.

Until recent years all man's activities have been regulated by his natural environment. The Forest of Dean and the Lower Wye Valley have been the scene of feverish activity for over 2000 years, reaching a peak in the 19th century. Subsequently other regions developed the skills and resources for which 'Dean' had always been famous.

Sitting like a great saucer in a hollow in the old Red Sandstone is a

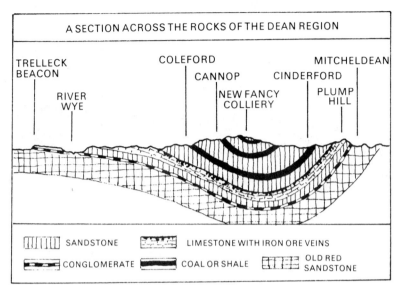

A SECTION ACROSS THE ROCKS OF THE DEAN REGION

TRELLECK BEACON — COLEFORD — MITCHELDEAN
CANNOP — CINDERFORD
RIVER WYE — NEW FANCY COLLIERY — PLUMP HILL

| | SANDSTONE | | LIMESTONE WITH IRON ORE VEINS |
| | CONGLOMERATE | | COAL OR SHALE | | OLD RED SANDSTONE |

layer of very hard conglomerate rock – nature's concrete. On this is a pile of other saucers – some of hard rock, some of soft, some thick but some very thin. Working up the pile from the conglomerate, the next five are different sorts of limestone. Then there is one of hard sandstone, followed by some 32 made up alternately of soft sandstone and coal. The whole pile has been weathered away so that there is hardly anything left of the top saucers. Walks 11 to 18 have been planned to go over the exposed edges of many of these saucers, which in some cases are only a few inches thick. Over millions of years the pile of saucers has become irregular and the eastern edges now come up to the surface nearly vertically, whilst the western edges have been pushed down. To the east on Plump Hill (Walk 18) it is possible to walk over the edges of a dozen saucers in five minutes but on the western side it is sometimes two or three miles between rock changes.

Books which have more information on the region are: *Forestry Commission Guide, Dean Forest and Wye Valley*, HMSO; Dreghorn W., *Geology Explained in the Forest of Dean and Wye Valley*, David & Charles.

On Charcoal Burning

Charcoal burning is one of the oldest occupations of man. Only when the technique had been mastered could prehistoric man make use of bronze, glass and later iron. Charcoal was as essential to the armies of Achilles as it was to those of Cromwell and it was not until the 18th century that its importance gradually declined.

Wood does not burn at a high enough temperature to melt metals, but by a process of enclosed burning the impurities can be driven off,

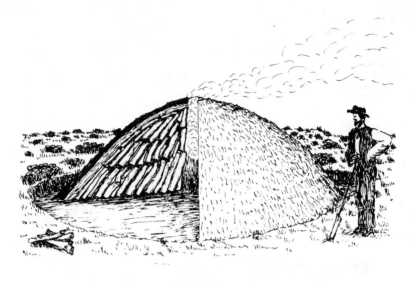

A CHARCOAL PIT

leaving a residue of almost pure carbon. Charcoal fires, especially when given plenty of air, are much hotter than wood or coal, as can be seen at a barbecue.

First came the woodcutters who prepared stacks of timber made up of the limbs of trees, underwood and coppice. These stacks were left for some months to dry. Then came the charcoal burners grouping their pits as near as was convenient to the stacks of timber. Once a pit was fired another nearby was prepared, so that at any one time up to six pits were in various stages of use. A stack took about three days to build and then at least three days to burn. It needed constant attention to prevent the blow holes in the soil covering getting out of control.

The pit was made by first excavating a circular hearth about six inches deep and 16 feet in diameter. The short poles of wood were then stacked three or four layers high, leaving a hole down the centre. Finally the whole dome except the hole at the top was covered with a layer of bracken or leaves and sealed with the earth which had been excavated earlier. To ignite the wood, burning charcoal was shovelled into the hole at the top, which was then sealed. To regulate the burning, small holes were poked in the sides of the dome where required. In windy weather screens were erected to prevent the burning taking place too quickly. (These screens were called 'loos'.) About $1\frac{1}{4}$ tons of wood produced about $\frac{1}{4}$ ton of charcoal and all the by-products, such as creosote and tar, were wasted.

The charcoal burner lived a lonely, ever moving life. His possessions were few and his comforts small. His only shelter in the forest was a 'bovey' or small tent made of poles and covered with bracken – not the most luxurious accommodation for the many months spent away from home.

Walk 1   St Pierre's Great Wood

$3\frac{1}{2}$ miles (5·5 km)

OS sheet 162

St Pierre's Great Wood is set on high ground overlooking the Severn where it is joined by the Wye. What is usually a conflict between timber farming and recreation has here been skilfully moulded together. The rotation of crops, which give variety to the eye, are seen at their best from the well laid out and maintained paths. The edges of these paths and the forest roads are full of wild flowers and shrubs which are the homes of innumerable insects and their predators, the birds. It is an excellent walk for observing natural history.

The wood is best reached from the large roundabout on the southern outskirts of Chepstow, one mile from junction 22 on the M4. From this roundabout take the A48 road to Caerwent and Newport. In one mile look for a turning on the right opposite the New Inn, sign-posted to Shirenewton, and in a further $\frac{1}{4}$ mile fork left. The small parking area is $\frac{1}{2}$ mile along this lane on the left.

Leave the car park by the only way into the wood and follow the forest walk. Wind through the young wood and pass a turning on the right. You will come back down here. After you have been walking for $\frac{1}{4}$ mile turn left along a forest road. Forests and woods are farmed just as other parts of the countryside are. Areas which correspond to the arable farmer's fields are laid out and when there are only mature trees it is clear-felled. Everything is cut down. Then starts a cycle which may last for 200 years. Trees are planted in rows to give the maximum number to the acre. When they have grown to form a dense canopy overhead they are thinned out, allowing those that remain to mature. There are many ways of cropping the ground. One type of tree may be left to grow for 150 years, whilst others may be replaced every 40 years. There are at least a dozen types of conifers (those bearing cones) and half a dozen broadleaves (known as hardwoods). They are planted bearing in mind, amongst other factors, the type of soil, the market and the need to make the woods attractive to look at. On this and other walks in the book you will be able to appreciate some of the work of the forester.

As you walk down the forest road you may notice how the birds use the stones, which show from time to time in the roadway, as anvils on which to crack the snail shells. 30 yards after the first bend in the forest road there is a sign on the left which says Llwybr Cyhoeddus or public footpath. Turn left and go down this very attractive path.

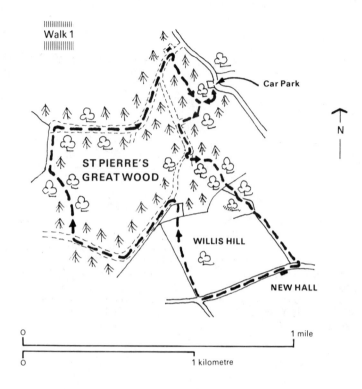

Car Park

N

ST PIERRE'S
GREAT WOOD

WILLIS HILL

NEW HALL

0   1 mile

0   1 kilometre

Between the next two stiles, a distance of about 200 yards, there are at least 29 different wild flowers, not counting bushes and grasses. How many can you identify?

Go over the first stile and in 8 paces cross an 'Animal Trunk Road'. Look to the right and you see the track winding away into the distance; to the left it goes under the bushes into the dark wood. As you go down the path there are more of these cross tracks. This is a natural wood. Here we humans fit in better because it is the home of animals. It is in such a place that the sense of being part of the natural world, which all of us seek who go out into the countryside, can be most easily found. After the second stile continue ahead to a gate in the fence on the right. From this gate turn left and go down the field. In 100 yards, when the ridge on the right ends, bear right up to the far corner where there is a gate. In the next field go forward for 10 yards and then over a stile in the hedge on the left. Now turn right and follow first the hedge and then a fence, to a stile leading on to a lane. Turn right and pass a farm on the left.

The lane now becomes a hedged track. These hedges are probably 550 to 600 years old, and the one on the left may have been the edge of a wood. The age of a hedge can usually be found by counting the number of species growing in thirty-metre lengths, taking the average and multiplying by a hundred. Where there are predominantly woodland species the hedge may have once formed part of a wood or there may have been a wood nearby. Continue to where the track joins a lane. Here turn right through a gate and walk with the old fence posts and hawthorn trees on your left. In 200 yards you will see the wood ahead with two entrances. Go to the one on the right where there is another footpath notice. Walk on into the wood to the forest road and turn left.

On the right the hillside has been clear-felled and replanted again. Continue along the forest road which goes just inside the wood so that you may catch glimpses of the Severn estuary three miles away. At the bend, at the time of writing, the climbing travellers joy has smothered the trees, weighing them down so that some have died. When the path starts to go uphill the rather fine trees planted here are western hemlock, which gets its name from the early American settlers who found the crushed needles smelt like the wild flower called hemlock. The tree grows wild on the west coast of North America, where it is found in the heavy shade of the Douglas fir and red cedar forests. At the end of the dark wood on the right there is a footpath. Here turn right up the hill. The younger plantation on the left has not yet formed a canopy so the wild flowers and shrubs are flourishing. In a few years' time the light will be cut off and nothing will grow under the trees, but the seeds are all there and as soon as the trees are removed there will again be a mass of wild flowers.

At the top of the hill cross an overgrown track and in 100 yards bear right, just inside the wood, to a clearing. Here there is a view over the fields to the left. Turn right along a grass track. From August to November this is a popular place for collecting fungi. Many that you find are edible and are in fact much more tasty than the shop mushrooms, but a few are poisonous. So unless you know what you are doing, leave well alone. Continue with the main track for one mile. When you see a foresters' lean-to store shed on the left, turn right down a narrow grass path. This takes you down to a 'T' junction, where you turn left back to the car.

Walk 2 Chepstow

5½ miles (9 km)

OS sheet 162*

Chepstow is the gateway to the Wye Valley. The name given to it by the Britons was Castell Gwent and today it is still known to the Welsh by the shortened version Cas Gwent. Though the Normans called it Stiguil, the name did not stick and it soon reverted to the one given to it by the Saxons – Cheapstow or 'market town'. The castle, as we know it today, was started soon after the Norman Conquest and the town grew rapidly under its walls. Strongbow, the conqueror of Ireland, was born in the castle and later it played an important role in the Civil War. The Portwall, which was built to protect the civilian population, now cuts right through the town but originally it formed the southern limit. The nearby crossing of the Severn at Beachley, called the Old Passage, had always been a chancy business until the road bridge was completed in 1966.

Cars can be parked in the Portwall car park at the upper end of the town centre. It is well signposted near the Portwall Gate in the main street. The walk starts from that part of the car park which overlooks the castle.

Go through a small doorway in the Portwall into a childrens playground which overlooks the dry ditch round the castle. In 200 yards you come to the main B4235 road out of Chepstow to the north and west. Turn right and walk along the road for ¼ mile, passing the Mount School on the left, and at the second turning on the right, turn right. This has a small sign on the bank on the left which says 'Wye Valley Walk'. For the next 1½ miles there will be yellow arrows to guide the way. In 50 yards, at the beginning of a row of trees, there is an arrow pointing to the left. Follow this direction down the path, past the buildings and then across the playing fields. On the far side there is a stile in the boundary fence. Here the path goes down the hill to the right, between the fence and a high park wall, to a stile at the end of the wall. The path is well used and very well waymarked, so for the next mile keep to the path.

As you walk along you go through a yew wood. These trees were common in the Welsh marches in the Middle Ages. But it is incorrect to suppose that it was from such trees as these that the famous Welsh archers obtained their bows. The best longbows have always been made of yew but other woods such as ash and elm do good service. The English yew grows slowly and the branches are close together,

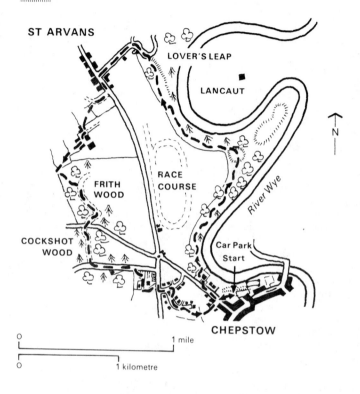

therefore the wood is full of knots. The archers at Agincourt used bows made from yew staves which were imported from the Continent where they grew faster and with fewer knots. Chepstow was a centre for the import of yew staves in exchange for Dean iron and Welsh leather.

After climbing up to the earthworks of a small fort, there are very good views down through the trees to the Lancant bend. On the left was a great house called Piercefield, now in ruins, but its park is a fine setting for Chepstow race course. $\frac{1}{2}$ mile past the fort the path forks. The right fork is a continuation of the Wye Valley Walk and it goes past some impressive cliffs. You now leave the yellow arrows and fork left to zigzag up to the top of the cliffs and continue at a higher level. If you had followed the arrows you would soon have come to the Giant's Cave. All caves seem to have been the homes of giants and this one no doubt enjoyed a cave with a view.

Continue along the top path with periodical glimpses of the Wye far

15

below on the right and a field on the left. In $\frac{1}{4}$ mile the path comes to 'Lovers Leap'. Keep children under complete control and anyone who has not a head for heights should pursue a route a few yards to the left, away from the edge of the precipice. Walk on out to the A466 Chepstow–Monmouth road. Turn left along the grass verge and when it ends cross the road and face the oncoming traffic. Pass the turning to Wyndcliff and in a few yards join the pavement. This takes you to St Arvans. At the road junction you may admire the circular drinking fountain, with its water-boys and dolphins, but no water. Until this century the main road from Chepstow to Monmouth came down the Devauden road, though a road up the valley through Tintern had developed since the 17th century.

Turn towards Chepstow and pass the Piercefield Inn on the right. In 100 yards, opposite a turnpike milestone set in the wall, turn right through a gate on to a concrete road, signposted Cophill, 2 km. When the road bears right through a gate to a sewage works, keep straight on along the edge of the field and go through a gate – and admire the fact that it works. On this farm all is clean and tidy. From the gate go across the field to the nearside corner of the farm buildings and turn left through a gate. At the far end of the building turn right into the farmyard. Turn left past the house and then turn right between the buildings to a gate. Now go straight across the field and from the next gate the right-of-way bears left to the bottom right-hand corner of the wood on the left. It is not difficult to go round the field to the left if there is a standing crop. In the bottom corner of the field go through a hunting gate and turn left. In 10 yards turn left into Fryth Wood. Follow the track up through the wood and at the forest road turn right. On the left there are some tall piles of pine needles and at the time of writing one is some four feet high. These are wood ant nests.

On reaching the parking area beyond the barrier turn right, pass the sign 'Rhodfa'r goedwig' and continue out to the road. Cross this and enter Cockshoot Wood. Follow the forest road for $\frac{1}{4}$ mile to the B4235 road from Chepstow to Usk. Cross the road and turn left along the narrow grass verge. In $\frac{1}{4}$ mile 50 yards past the end of a garden on the right, there is a stile into a field on the right. Go over this and bear left as if to cross in front of the new Forensic Science Laboratory. At the boundary fence turn right and follow it up the hill to a field. Turn left and continue with the fence on the left to the road. Cross the road and turn right towards Chepstow.

In 100 yards turn left along Kings Mark Lane. In just over 100 yards turn right and follow the footpath sign down to the end of an estate road. At the other end of the short road you will find that this is St John's Gardens. Turn left and follow the road down for nearly $\frac{1}{4}$ mile to bear right along a path to the right of the end house. This takes you along the valley to the end of a wide entry between houses and so out again to the B4235 road out of Chepstow. Cross to the children's playground and at the far end go through the doorway in the Portwall into the car park.

Walk 3   Chepstow Park Wood

3 miles (5 km)

OS sheets 162 & 171(*)

Chepstow Park Wood is four miles northwest of Chepstow. It lies on the south side of the B4293. If you are travelling from St Arvans and the A466, the Forestry Commission car park is on the left, almost opposite a turning to Tintern and the Cot.

Walk back out of the car park across the road and between two gateposts into New Wood. Keep straight ahead and go down a sunken track to the enlarged end of the forest road. This is where the foresters sort out the timber ready for dispatch. Go straight over this area and continue down the track. On reaching the edge of the wood the track goes on down with a field on the right for 50 yards. Do not fork left where the horses go, for this will eventually take you back into the wood. Continue past the side of the cottage and on down the entrance track to a lane. Bear right and in 100 yards the lane crosses a brook. Just beyond here look on the left for the entrance to an old lane, no longer needed to be maintained for its full length. The first 20 yards, that part which crosses the grass verge, may be rather overgrown but when the canopy of leaves from the two hedges cuts out the light, the grasses, nettles and brambles cease to grow. This old road is some-times stony, sometimes a grass track and sometimes a tarred lane.

    At the top of the hill, where the stony section ends, there is a barn on the left which has seen better days. The narrow slits in the walls, put there to keep the contents free from mould, are exactly the same as those found in castles. Could this barn have been built before castles became obsolete, when the castle-building tradition was still active? Continue along the old road for a further $\frac{3}{4}$ mile to walk along the side of the Masons' Arms and so into the village of Devauden.

    Cross the road and pass the modern village hall on the left. At the end of the wire fence turn left up a wide hedged track, signposted 'Itton 2·9 km'. On reaching the wood you have a choice of four ways. Go along the second from the left, that is to say you bear left. This way turns into a sunken track as it slowly climbs up the hillside. On the banks of the track grow two types of fern, the short hard fern and the taller male fern.

    This is an ideal place for observing the wood ant at work. The tall mound of tiny bits of wood and pine needles represent many ant-hours of work. Thousands of these insects can be seen struggling with gigantic loads from the floor of the track, up the almost vertical bank

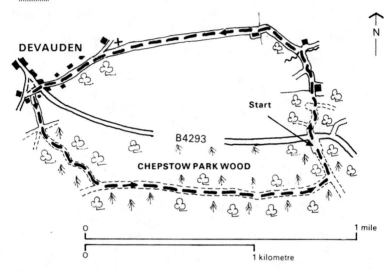

and then to the top of the mound – a distance of some six feet. Size for size this would be like a man carrying a wardrobe up 1000 feet of quarry face. If you stand very still you can sometimes hear the faint rustle of thousands of feet on the dry leaves under the trees.

On reaching the forest road bear left along the road. Here there is a mixture of trees along the edge. As summer progresses you will be able to find evidence of the gall wasp. There are a number of different small winged or wingless insects in this family and each one produces a different type of gall. Look under some of the oak leaves and you will find small red pills, larger orange ones and large yellow marbles. Perhaps at the end of a stalk, where there should be a small bud, there is a large swelling which looks like a small artichoke. Again on another stalk there may be a pink furry ball. These are all galls, produced by the tree to encapsulate the egg of the gall wasp.

In $\frac{1}{2}$ mile the track goes downhill and for the next 200 yards there is, down near the ditch on the right, a mass of hair moss. Continue down this forest road to the 'T' junction and turn left to the start of the walk.

5½ miles (9 km)

OS sheet 162*

Fedw Wood (pronounced Faidoe) is four miles northwest of Chepstow. It lies on the north side of the B4293, the right side if travelling from Chepstow. The entrance to the Forestry Commission car park is two miles from the race course.

The walk is through woods and farmland. There is one short steep hill to climb but the other slopes are gentle.

The walk starts out from the car park along the forest road which is opposite the entrance. For a short while it follows the forest trail. Continue along the forest road for ½ mile until you come to a gate at the end of the wood. Go through this and along a hedged track which soon joins a farm road. In a few yards go over a fence on the left and walk up the field next to the hedge on the right. Many old tracks had footpaths which ran parallel to them. Until the advent of motorised transport, clean, smooth road surfaces were not essential. So while the horse and cart went up the muddy lane the passengers – who had to get out and walk on most of the hills – went up the adjoining pasture.

Leave the field in the corner and go out to the 'T' junction. Turn left and in ten yards go through a gate on the right, to follow the footpath signposted 'Tintern 2·2 km'. Head for a point in the hedge on the left about 100 yards from the road. As you cross the field you will see through a gap in the hedge that there is a small church, standing alone just across a small field. Go to the left of the churchyard to a stone stile. Continue with the wall on the right and when it ends bear very slightly right across a large field. As you cross the field some buildings ¼ mile away will come into view through a gap in the hedge. From the gate in this gap go down the field to the opposite corner and pass to the left of the farm to a track. Here turn left. The next farm along the track is Penterry Farm. Pass straight through and then through a gate across the track at the end of a barn on the right. Turn right past the end of the barn to pass a house on the left. At the end of the derelict building attached to the house turn left and go down the bank towards a wood. Look into the wood for a path at a point in line with the end of the derelict building. You may have to walk along the field looking into the wood, before you see the well-used path inside the wood. Follow this path down through the trees for 100 yards and then fork left, which takes you on down. At the forest road bear right and in a few yards go left to a continuation of the path. When the path goes

19

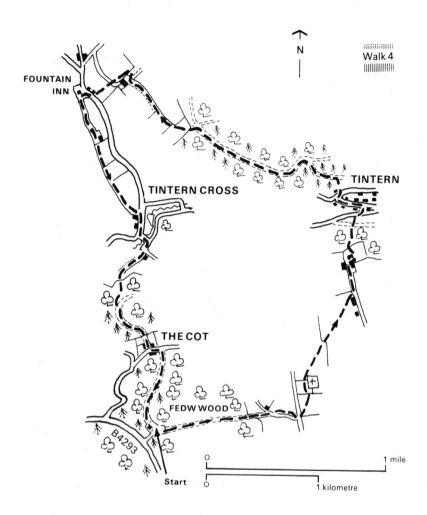

between banks, take care, as you will suddenly emerge on to a lane.

Turn right along the lane and in 20 yards, turn left to follow the footpath sign down to the Forge Road. As the name implies, this was once a busy industrial centre. The night sky would be aglow from the charcoal furnace fires and the quiet would be disturbed by the constant clanging of hammer against iron. A spot $\frac{1}{4}$ mile up the valley is still marked on maps as 'old furnace'. At the lane turn left and go down to the road junction. Here turn right as if to go down the valley but turn left in 10 yards, through a gap in the hedge. This path climbs steeply to a forest road. After you have rested awhile, walk up the forest road, which climbs gradually up the side of the valley.

This very pleasant forest road is part of a nature trail which starts in Tintern, so when an arrow points along a track to the right, ignore it. After $\frac{3}{4}$ mile you come to a crossing of ways. From here you get your first view of a field over a hedge to the left. Bear left down a grass track to a gate which has a stile on the right. You now have to cross this field, so aim for the house in the distance which is painted completely white. In 200 yards you will be walking with a hedge on the right. This path soon turns into a farm track. Keep to the hedge on the right through an old orchard to a gate into a farmyard. A little way inside the yard turn right out of the yard. Now bear left to a stile in the hedge on the left. The right of way goes across the next field, then across the farm road. But in the interest of the farmer, and also because the next two stiles are overgrown, keep to the left of the field past the farm buildings, to a gate in the corner. Go straight ahead and through a gate into a field and bear right down towards the Fountain Inn. You may have seen the inn sign from time to time after you left the wood. There is a stile in the bottom hedge opposite the inn.

Behind the small car park at the side of the inn a grass hedged track can be seen. This used to be an important road down to Tintern Cross. In winter the lower road was more difficult and this was the Monmouth to Chepstow main road before the Turnpike Trust opted for the longer route through Devauden. This in its turn was superseded by the A466 through Redbrook and Tintern. At the lane turn right and follow it round the valley to the road junction. You will see on the left one of the ponds which supplied water to work the furnace bellows.

Turn left over the bridge and then right, following the footpath sign. Pass below a cottage and keep ahead to a sunken track going up the bank. At the top of the field where another grass track crosses, bear left up to a gate into a wood. Follow the old track through the wood, rising gently and keeping the same general direction. Cross the first forest road but bear right along the second. Keep to this for nearly $\frac{1}{2}$ mile, to the end of the forest. Go through a gate and straight ahead on a track with a tall hedge on the left. In $\frac{1}{4}$ mile this will bring you to the Cot, belonging to the Forestry Commission. At the lane turn left. In 100 yards look for a footpath sign on the right. A few yards past the sign, turn right and follow the forest road back to the car park.

Walk 5   Tintern

5 miles (8 km)

OS sheet 162*

The development of Tintern took place in three stages. The arrival of
the Cistercians in 1131 put the vale of Tintern on the map. The
Cistercians had to settle for the isolated north and west because so
much of south and east England was already in ecclesiastical hands.
This efficient organisation obtained a large area of hill lands on which
to develop its sheep production, in a district where the indigenous
farmer specialised in cattle farming. With their expertise and ready
markets through the parent house in Europe, the venture flourished.
At the end of the 13th century they had 2300 head of sheep. According
to the Little Red Book of Bristol they had the edge over their com-
petitors in the 14th century as they enjoyed freedom from toll
'throughout the lands of the King of England' – even though their
wool was described as 'of the worst quality'. Gradually their fortunes
diminished and they were suppressed along with the lesser
monasteries.

The second stage started thirty years after the suppression in 1566,
when William Humfres introduced German experts to Tintern and
started a wire drawing works. With an abundant supply of water from
the Fedw brook to provide power and a good tidal river on which to
transport the finished goods, Tintern became a centre of the iron
industry. It was only gradually that the economies of steam power
and the rise of the South Wales valleys forced most of the forges to
close during the 19th century.

The third stage began with the motor car. The beauty of the setting
and the remains of the first 'boom-town' attract numerous visitors
who are gradually leaving their mark on the countryside.

This walk is to the top of the hill opposite the Abbey car park and
then along Offa's Dyke. In some places it may be muddy from the
heavy traffic of walking boots and in one place it is rather stony.

Tintern is four miles north of Chepstow on the A446 road. It is eight
miles south of Monmouth and well signposted from all directions.
The walk starts from the car park next to the Abbey ruins.

Leave the car park and go to the riverside. Turn left and follow the
path between the houses, passing the new bungalows on the right
which were built on the old quay. At the main road turn right past the
shops and then by a stone wall. Look over the wall at the rusting water
wheel. At the end of the wall turn right and cross the river. This bridge

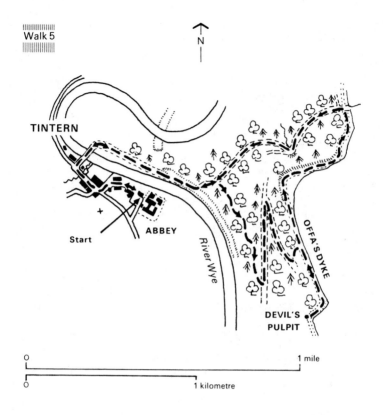

N

TINTERN

Start

ABBEY

River Wye

OFFA'S DYKE

DEVIL'S
PULPIT

0   1 mile

0   1 kilometre

was built in 1876 to connect the Tintern wire works with the newly opened Chepstow to Monmouth railway. Coal could now supplement waterpower. On plaques near the centre of the bridge is the inscription 'Isca Foundry Co. . . . Newport' – an indication that industry was moving south. (This firm also made the Old Pier at Weston-Super-Mare in 1867.) Follow the track, being careful not to trip over the old sleepers. In 200 yards fork left where there is a stone track going up the hillside. Before the railways came, much of the cross country traffic was by pack horse or on the human back. Gradients which no normal motor vehicle would ever attempt seem to have been commonplace. It is no wonder that so many people did not live to old age, if they spent their time carrying heavy loads on tracks such as this. Nevertheless you go up this track to the fork.

To the left is Tintern Old Station. Fork right for Offa's Dyke and Devil's Pulpit. In a short distance you fork right again, following the yellow arrows. You will come back down the left fork. Continue along this track which goes along the hillside to rise up to a forest road. Here

23

turn left,. You are now just over 300 feet above the river but notice that the wild flowers on either side make it look as if you are in a midland water meadow. When the yellow arrows direct you round to the right on to another forest road, notice the bank of common horsetails on the right. Follow the yellow arrows on up the hillside to a 'T' junction with Offa's Dyke, Chepstow $9\frac{1}{2}$ miies to the right, Prestatyn 265 miles to the left.

The Devil's Pulpit is now $\frac{1}{2}$ mile up to the right but you will have to return to this point as the walk continues to the left. If you walk the $\frac{1}{2}$ mile to the viewpoint you will see a small square of rock jutting out from the hillside. It is almost completely surrounded by trees affording only a narrow view of the top of the opposite hillside. It is said that the Devil harangued the monks from this rock but it is not known if they heard, $\frac{3}{4}$ mile away down in the valley.

If you decide not to go to the Devil's Pulpit turn left along Offa's Dyke. This ancient earthwork stretches, with a gap in the Herefordshire plain, from north to south through the marches. It was the western boundary of the Saxon Kingdom of Mercia and was built, towards the end of the 8th century, by the most important king in Britain. Over more than seventy miles of broken and sometimes mountainous country its remains rarely fail to be visable from the west. It was a reminder to Celtic Britain not only of the position of the boundary, but also of the presence to the east of a most powerful king.

Continue walking along the Dyke for $\frac{1}{4}$ mile. Near the end of a short length of very stony path there is a fine view to the left over the Wye. Follow the well-trodden path for a further $\frac{1}{2}$ mile, as it starts to go downhill. On passing the end of a forest road the Dyke Path goes on down towards Brockweir, but you turn left down the forest road. It is now easy walking almost all the way back.

In $\frac{1}{4}$ mile the forest road, which has been curving round the hillside to the left, suddenly makes a right hand bend as it passes over a stream. There is a very pleasant rocky hollow on the left, with moss and ferns. Just past the bend, fork right downhill. In $\frac{1}{2}$ mile you encounter the track you followed on the way up. Retrace your steps down to the railway and so back across the bridge into Tintern.

Walk 6   Tidenham Chase

2½ miles (4 km)

OS sheet 162*

Tidenham Chase is a collection of woodlands connected with the large manor of Tidenham. The village of Tidenham is now only small but the parish is still large, stretching from beneath the Severn Bridge in the south almost to Tintern in the north. This walk starts on the parish boundary and explores Oakhill Wood and Little Meend. It is easy walking, though in places it may be a little muddy in wet weather.

The walk starts from a layby on the B4228 Chepstow–Coleford Road, two miles south of St Briavels and 4½ miles north of Chepstow. From Chepstow turn left off the A48(T) ¼ mile from the river bridge. The layby is a length of old road near the top of a hill at the north end of the woods.

Leave the parking place at the top end and cross the road on to a wide grass verge. Follow the road round the bend and in 100 yards bear right to enter Oakhill Wood. Go under the barrier, which is to stop cars driving all over the forest, and turn right on to a narrow grass path. As you go along you will notice that the pines have been interplanted with Sitka spruce. At the time of writing the natural woodland is still growing here but eventually much of it will be smothered by the dense canopy which the conifers will make. For a few years more you will still be able to see ash, oak, birch, mountain ash and sallow and the ground cover of bilberries and ling. From time to time there are views over the surrounding valleys to the gentle slopes of St Briavels and you will see the fields are mainly pasture. After nearly ½ mile you come to a 'T' junction and here turn left along a wider track. Now you will see wild rhododendrons on either side.

At the cross-tracks turn right. You may notice the great mounds of bark shavings at the side of the forest road. When the forester is thinning out a plantation he has a quantity of poles which are to be sold for fencing posts. These are often treated against rot before selling and this is done in large tanks in the wood yard. The bark must first be removed and this is best done whilst the wood is still in the forest. A job which used to be very laborious is now done with a mobile barking machine. The logs are fed in at one end and side-cutters gently rotate the log whilst stripping off the bark. This bark is shot out to one side, so it is not difficult to tell where the work was done.

As the forest road starts to go downhill there is a young plantation

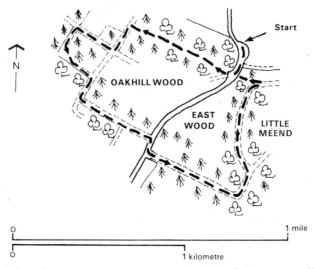

on the left and an even younger one on the right. It is easy to tell the age of the pines here because they make a whorl of branches on the trunk each year. The total growth for each year takes place between May and July and from then on the tree works at making next year's growth, in miniature, inside the bud. The next May the bud opens and the year's growth is unfolded. To tell the age from seed, count the whorls. Those on the left started in 1970. $\frac{1}{4}$ mile from the cross-tracks turn left on to a narrow grass path, with the old plantation on the right. In 100 yards bear left across the more open plantation to go along by the side of a beech and oak wood.

On reaching the 'T' junction turn right. Here there are more rhododendrons with a few sweet chestnuts. In about 200 yards when you can see a bend in the track ahead, turn left along a grass track which may be muddy in places. Here again there are hardwoods – oak, beech and chestnut on the right. There is an interesting collection of grasses on this track. Walk on out to the road.

Turn right and in 50 yards cross the road into East Wood. Walk on along the main track for $\frac{1}{4}$ mile and go round a left-hand bend. In a further 50 yards fork left. This track takes you through the woods known as Little Meend. In $\frac{1}{4}$ mile, at the top of the rise, the trees on the right open out a little and the track goes round a bend to the right. Three quarters of the way round this bend turn back to the left on to a narrow but good stone path. This will take you out to the road opposite the entrance to Oakhill Wood. Cross the road and turn right along the grass verge back to the car.

Walk 7   Trelleck Beacon

3½ miles (5·5 km)

OS sheet 162*

Trelleck was an important stage on the Monmouth–Chepstow road, which took the higher and dryer ground before the modern road down the valley was made. The three standing stones and the tumulus testify to the importance of the site to early man. The three standing stones, made of pebbly sandstone were part of a large long barrow and were erected nearly 5000 years ago. The tumulus is one of many in the borderland and it has been suggested that there are more in the Welsh marches because there have been less changes than in eastern and central parts of Britain. The third place mentioned by the local guide books is the Virtuous Well, a chalybeate spring now little more than a mud patch.

The village of Trelleck is on the B4293 about midway between Chepstow and Monmouth. It can also be reached from Llandogo by a somewhat steep and narrow lane.

The car can be parked at a small picnic site, ¾ mile east of Trelleck, on the edge of the wood. The site looks down across the fields to the village, from a road which runs parallel to the main street. It can be reached from either end of the village.

Go up the path at the back of the picnic area following the directions for the forest walk. On the right as you go up are the low bushes of bilberry, sometimes called whortleberry, huckleberry or whinberry. The small dark blue fruit are edible but they also make a good dye. They only grow on very acid soils so are usually found on mountain tops. At the junction with a track, turn right along the side of the hill. The track soon goes round to the left through more open ground. Follow this as far as the cross-tracks next to the wood. Now turn right and continue in the same direction for ½ mile. At a 'T' junction, with cleared ground in front, turn left. In 50 yards bear right through a gap in the wall to follow the path on the other side of the wall. After ¼ mile the well-used track turns left at cross-tracks. Go straight ahead through the trees to a lane and cross it to a small metal gate opposite. In the field bear slightly right, aiming a little to the right of a tall stone pillar which is a part of the disused entrance to Cleddon Hall. Here a metal gate leads on to another lane. Turn left and in ¼ mile take the first turn on the right. This lane goes down and over a stream to curve round a house on the left. At the end of the lane go along a narrow walled path to a 'T' junction.

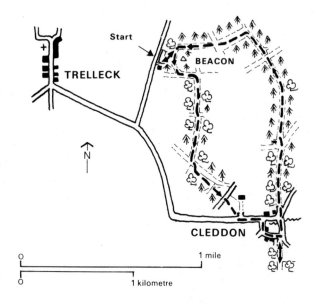

Here you are recommended to walk ½ mile to the right to Bargain Wood where there are fine views over the Wye Valley. You must return to this point and go along the level track. In a few yards you are at the top of Cleddon Shoots, a picturesque series of waterfalls which go down 750 feet to Llandogo. There is a steep path down at the side of the falls, which are best seen after heavy rain. Cross the road and continue on the track, climbing steadily. This is part of the Wye Valley Walk, a well-marked path from Chepstow to Symonds Yat.

In ½ mile when the path looks as if it might level out, there is a fork. Go left on to a forest road. Cross straight over and follow the forest walk up the hill. This grass track gradually levels out. After nearly ½ mile it comes to a well-used stony track. Cross straight over on to a grass path. In a few yards keep straight ahead along a path used by horses. This is marked by a short post with an orange top on which is burnt a horseshoe. In ¼ mile turn left up a track lined with masses of bilberries. At the next crossing go straight over on to a track which stretches away into the distance. The track eventually curves round to the left as it goes round Trelleck Beacon. Without the trees which now cover the whole hilltop, this place would give wonderful views, as it is the highest point for many miles around. It stands 1005 feet above sea level. Continue on a 200 yard length of straight track and at the next bend bear right. This is the path down to the car park.

28

Walk 8   Newland

5½ miles (9 km)

OS sheet 162*

The river Wye has not always followed exactly the same course that it does today. In its early days it meandered over a plain, making its leisurely way to the sea. Then the level of the plain gradually rose, causing the river to speed up and cut deeper into its bed. This walk follows one of the ancient meanders. It must have been much the same as the one at Sellack (Walk 25) at one time, but early in its life it cut through the neck of land at Redbrook. Since then the river has continued to cut its way deeper and deeper, so that now it is nearly 400 feet lower than its fossil meander.

Newland is three miles southeast of Monmouth and six miles northwest of Lydney. It lies on the B4231 about two miles from the A466 at Redbrook.

Cars should be parked close to the edge of the road at the side of the churchyard, not along the main road which tends to be rather narrow. The side road has in it a fine row of almshouses, founded in 1615 and recently restored.

Leave the village along the main road towards Redbrook, passing the Ostrich Inn on the right. A little beyond the end of the farm buildings on the left, at the end of the village turn left at the footpath sign. From the stile bear right and cross the field towards the left-hand end of the wood on the hill ¼ mile away. As you go over the field you will see a gate in the angle of the hedge. Bear left and go through the gate and up the next field near the hedge on the left. Pass a gate on the left and at the top of the ridge go over a fence on the left and walk with the hedge now on the right. Continue through three more fields. In the second field there is a spring a short way up the field but above the spring it is quite dry. In the third field, go over the stile in the far corner. Now turn left to walk next to a fence. At the end of the fence go over a stile. Keep straight ahead, with the wood on the right, and when the wood ends bear slightly right to a point in the hedge 30 yards to the left of an electricity pole. Go down through the bushes to a stile and follow the path on through the wood. At the bottom of the wood there is a stile into a field. Turn left just outside the wood and when the wood ends, continue across the field to the left of the white house seen across the valley. From a stile go down to cross the stream by the footbridge and so up on to the road – but take care, children should be under complete control.

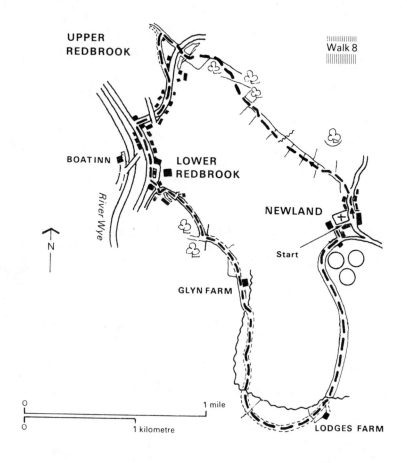

UPPER REDBROOK

BOAT INN

LOWER REDBROOK

River Wye

N

NEWLAND

Start

GLYN FARM

O   1 mile

O   1 kilometre

LODGES FARM

To avoid walking down the narrow winding road to the left, go over the road and up a steep track, waymarked Offa's Dyke Path. On reaching the far end of a whitened stone cottage turn left through a small wooden gate. Cross the grass and go down the stone roadway. As you go down there is a good view over to the left of the remains of one of the Forest of Dean industrial estates! It started with a furnace in the 17th century which was followed by a stamping mill and foundry, all using vast quantities of charcoal and water. On reaching the road continue, facing the oncoming traffic. The bridge with the sloping top was where a tramway from Lower Redbrook tinplate works went up to the GWR forest railway. Just before reaching the bottom of the hill, about 20 yards from the Bush Inn, there are a few remains of a copper works, which flourished from 1690 to 1730. The ore was brought from Cornwall to Chepstow and then up to the Wye,

30

providing a return load for the otherwise empty boats. The building was later enlarged for a tinplate works which spread out to where the garage now stands.

At the main road turn left past the Wye Valley Petrol Station and Café. Continue along the main road, bear left at the island garage and go round behind it. On your left is the entrance to another 17th century copper works, later the Lower Redbrook tinplate works and now a waste paper firm's depot. Go up the long flight of steps, way-marked Offa's Dyke Path and at the top turn left. Follow the road round to the right, ignoring the right fork up to the houses. Go to the end of the road and then fork right along a stone track. This track has a base of burnt limestone and clinker from the local furnaces. In $\frac{1}{4}$ mile the main track turns round to the right but here turn left to a gate. As you walk down this track you can see Forge Cottage down below on the left. Continue to Glyn Farm and go through the gate next to the house. Keep straight ahead past the farm equipment stores and cross the brook in 200 yards. This track goes up the valley, eventually cross-ing back over the brook. In $\frac{3}{4}$ mile the track joins the road to Lodges Farm and crosses the brook by an attractive stone bridge – they don't build them like that any more.

Keep ahead for another $\frac{3}{4}$ mile. At the beginning of Newland turn left uphill. At the top of the hill turn right back to the car.

Walk 9

Moseley Green

$3\frac{1}{2}$ miles (5·5 km)

OS sheet 162*

This walk goes through the forest to Parkend which was, until recently, an important coal producing centre. All that is left now is the truncated Severn and Wye railway line to Lydney from the coalfields around Cinderford and Speech House.

Moseley Green is $1\frac{1}{2}$ miles northeast of Parkend. It can best be reached from the B4431 Coleford to Blakeney road by turning along a sideroad which is signposted Yorkley at The Barracks. In $\frac{1}{4}$ mile this side road passes a small cluster of houses with the Rising Sun Inn standing well back from the road. Opposite the houses an old railway went into a tunnel and the road winds over the entrance. Here, under the trees, is a short curved track on the left, with parking for a few cars. The walk starts from here.

Leave the car park and go towards the houses and the Rising Sun. Walk along the rough ground between the houses and the wood on the left, climbing up to a small pool at the side of the Rising Sun. Bear left up to an opening in the wood. Just inside there is a meeting of four grass paths. Go straight across and then bear right up the hill. In 50 yards bear left and on up to a forest road. Continue straight ahead along this road and in 100 yards turn left. This is Church Hill and this part of the forest has become Churchill Inclosure. No doubt in years to come stories of the great abandoned coal mines will become connected with the 1939–45 war – this is the stuff that legends are made from. At the cross-tracks keep on in the same direction leaving Churchill Lodge on the right.

As you walk through the woods you may disturb two distinct species of birds, which fly up from the path 50 yards ahead and announce your approach to all and sundry. One is the magpie and the other the jay. The magpie can easily be recognised, as it appears in the distance to be black and white. The jay, though it too is partly black and white, has a brown look about the body. The magpie is larger (18 ins) than the jay ($13\frac{1}{2}$ ins) but the jay makes the worst noise, a harsh scolding screech. It will often make this blood-curdling noise from a tree in the wood as you pass.

Continue straight ahead to the road. On the left are the remains of one of the forest giants. It was called the School Oak from the school on the other side of the road. Turn right and go down the road. At the bottom of the hill go past the level crossing gate on the left and just

32

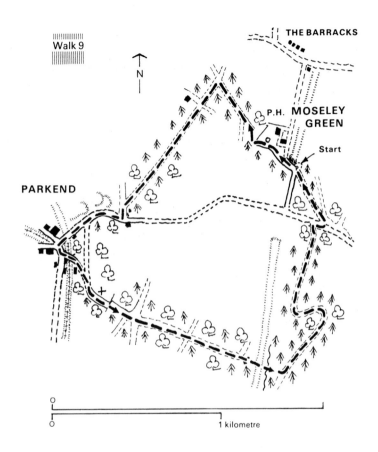

THE BARRACKS

P.H. MOSELEY
GREEN

Start

PARKEND

N

0

0   1 kilometre

beyond it is a Free Miners' coal yard. At the crossroads turn left. Here is the end of the only railway line left in Dean. Until 1977 it was the headquarters of the Dean Forest Railway Preservation Society, but then the society moved three miles down the Lydney road to a larger site. Turn left across the railway by the footbridge and go up the hill past the cottages to the church. Walk on into the forest and go down to a large forest road junction. There is now the choice of three forest roads and one smaller track. Go straight ahead up this track, which has been enlarged at the beginning by cutting away the high banks. Until recently the forester used horses to pull out the timber. Today the larger motorised vehicles need both wider and firmer surfaces on which to operate. This is one of the old horse tracks, as well as being an old road between Parkend and Yorkley. On the right are the remains of an old coppiced chestnut wood. There are many accounts of complaints against the charcoal burners, as it was alleged that they devastated the forest. No doubt, unsupervised in the depth of the forest, they sometimes exceeded their rights, but it was not in their own interest to destroy the woods. Their 'Coppicing' of hardwoods looked drastic for the first year because it cut all the trees down to a foot from the ground. It is in the nature of oaks and sweet chestnuts to have many dormant buds just below the bark, and when the tree is decapitated these epicormic buds, as they are called, send out new shoots. The numerous slender poles which then grow up from the stump were ideal for making charcoal but useless for the construction of timber houses and ships.

Cross straight over the next forest road. Keep children and dogs on the track here as there are old mine shafts in the woods and they are dangerous. Continue straight ahead to go down past a freeminers' mine and over the old railway embankment. After crossing the brook in the valley, climb up the hillside and cross an old track to arrive at a new forest road. Here turn left and gradually ascend round the head of the valley and then to the road. Bear right across the road to a wide grass clearing on the other side and turn left. You are now confronted with two grass tracks. Go along the left-hand one which takes you back to the car.

Walk 10

Blackpool Bridge

4 miles (6·5 km)

OS sheet 162*

(rather w. roads)

During the Roman occupation and probably for many years before that, the Forest of Dean provided iron for the armies of south and west Britain. The development of the heavy iron-clad plough lead to an increased demand for iron. Therefore roads had to be upgraded to take the increased traffic. This walk goes up the hill overlooking Lydney and returns for over a mile along a Roman road.

The Forestry Commission has provided many parking and picnic sites in the forest. Wench Ford is a good example of how this can be done without spoiling the environment. The car park is situated off the B4431, one mile northwest of Blakeney on the road to Parkend and Coleford. It can also be reached from the north by turning off the B4227 on a sharp bend south of Cinderford. The road through the forest is signposted to Blackpool Bridge and starts by going over a cattle grid.

There are two entrances to the car park. Use the northern one at Blackpool Bridge, next to the old railway bridge at the junction of the Cinderford road with the B4431. If you can, park near this end, as the walk comes back to this end of the car park.

Walk down the car park, passing the toilet block on the left, as far as the right-hand bend at the south end. The whole length of this park is set out on the bed of the ill-fated Forest of Dean Central Railway which ran from the New Fancy Colliery down to Awre Junction east of Blakeney. It was never completed at the northern end. (See Walk 11.)

At the bend turn left and go up a forest road for 200 yards. Turn right and in $\frac{1}{2}$ mile the forest road turns into a grass track. At the fork bear right downhill, passing a cottage on the left. At the lane turn right down the hill and round the bend. When the railings on the right end, turn back to the right downhill, past the Rudge on the right and a row of hawthorns on the left. This path will take you down to the main road. Bear right along the grass verge for 50 yards and cross the road to walk up a narrow lane.

20 yards up the lane fork right along a grass track which goes along the back of the houses at Pigeon Green. In 100 yards fork right again to a stile and gate. Continue climbing up the hill until you come to a gate at the top. Do not go through but turn right along a path which follows the wall on the left. In 200 yards, at a cross-track, turn left. In a

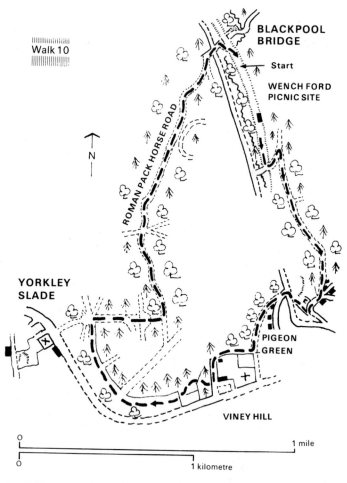

BLACKPOOL
BRIDGE

Start

WENCH FORD
PICNIC SITE

ROMAN PACK HORSE ROAD

N

YORKLEY
SLADE

PIGEON
GREEN

VINEY HILL

0   1 mile

0   1 kilometre

further 150 yards you come out on to the end of a lane near a cottage. Go down the lane and opposite the next house, about 100 yards before reaching the main road, turn right over a stile. Walk straight ahead and when you reach the disused pigeon loft bear right to a stile. This takes you to a narrow but well-trodden path through the trees. Beyond the next stile is more open land with well-spaced-out mature oak trees. Keep on ahead along tracks and paths, never very far from the woods on the right. Continue past two wide entrances to the forest when you will be able to keep company with a row of electricity poles. On reaching a meeting place of eight grass tracks and paths, you can either turn left for refreshment in Yorkley or turn right to continue the walk.

Go into the forest along the wide grass path. At the cross-tracks go straight over and on down to a very wide forest road. There are two ways into the trees opposite but take the right-hand one which is immediately in front of you. This goes straight down the hillside until it comes to a cross-track. To the right it goes gently downhill, and to the left it goes along the side of the hill. This is the Roman road. Turn left and follow it as it winds along the hillside. In nearly $\frac{1}{2}$ mile cross a small stream, usually little more than a muddy patch, and come to a cross path. Go straight ahead and gradually go down the hillside. In 50 yards a fallen tree may mean a small diversion to the left; this is how old paths get out of line over the years. When the Roman road goes up over a small rise, watch the surface for evidence of a stone causeway. Sometimes the edging stones, which were laid to form a raised curb, can be seen. At the bottom of the hill cross the main road and go along the road opposite towards Cinderford.

Pass under the old railway bridge and in 50 yards look in the grass verge on the left. You will see a length of the Roman road which has been fully exposed. Notice how it originally went down to the ford but later an addition was made to cross the bridge. This road left the Striguil (Chepstow) to Glevvm (Gloucester) road near Lydney and went up through Mitcheldean to Ariconium (near Weston-under-Penyard).

Return under the railway bridge and turn into Wench Ford.

Walk 11   Cannop Ponds

6½ miles (10.5 km)

OS sheet 162*

This walk is through the heart of the Forest of Dean. It includes three
of the best known 'Honeypots' and is full of interest. The start is from
the picnic site between two ponds and is reached from the B4226, 200
yards on the Cinderford side of the crossroads at Cannop. Look for the
Forestry Commission sign board at the bottom of the hill, and drive
down the long stone track starting next to the coal tip. Park anywhere
opposite the first pond.

Walk on along the track to the picnic area and at the end of the walk
you will come out of the wood opposite. There is now a choice of
routes. Either keep to the track along the old railway or follow the red
arrows across the picnic site and along the water-side path. These two
lakes were manmade in the early 19th century to store water for the
iron works at Parkend, just over a mile down the valley. At the end of
the lake a short digression across the dam brings you to the Forest of
Dean Stone Firm's yard.

It is here that stone from a quarry, high up on the other side of the
valley, is cut to various sizes. The stone is Pennant sandstone, known
as 'forest marble', and has three colours, yellow-brown when there is
limonite present, grey when carbonaceous material is mixed with the
sand grains, and blue when there is a variation of the other two or iron
sulphide is present. It is highly valued for building and was used for
University College of Wales, Aberystwyth; University College,
London; the Law Courts, London, and many other fine buildings. In
the quarry it is possible to find large casts of tree trunks (stigilleria),
some 280 million years old. One fine example, about four feet high, is
propped up on the right just inside the yard.

Return across the dam and go straight over the old railway. Do not
follow the yellow or red arrows which go to the left into a plantation
but bear right following a stone track just outside the plantation, with
an old oak wood on the right. In ¼ mile go straight over the cross-track
and then over a stile. Continue up the hill. At the junction of roads and
tracks go straight ahead up a narrow path. In ¼ mile join a forest road
and follow it to the main road. Turn left along the grass verge, taking
great care, as traffic tends to speed along this stretch.

In 200 yards cross the road and enter New Fancy car park. All
around are the waste tips of an old coal mine which have lately been
landscaped. On the right is a heap with a view. It is well worth the

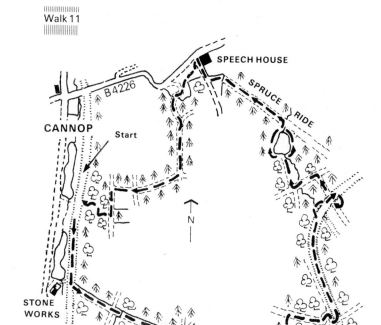

SPEECH HOUSE

SPRUCE RIDE

B4226

CANNOP

Start

N

STONE
WORKS

NEW
FANCY

0   1 mile

0   1 kilometre

climb up the path. Returning to the car park go towards the picnic place, passing the toilets hidden behind a bank on your right. Having turned left along an old railway track pass the picnic area on the left and you will come to a high wall on the left. This was part of the colliery buildings. You can see the old railway lines at the foot of the wall, which were in use until 1944 when the colliery closed. Opposite the far end of the wall there is a stile on the right. Go over this and immediately turn left along by a fence. As you go along the grass track you will see plenty of evidence of the old railway lines. This was the old shunting yard, on a slight gradient so that the loaded trucks could be sorted without the use of an engine.

On reaching the 'T' junction turn right down a very pleasant grass ride, bordered with a great variety of young trees. The sallow or goat willow predominates. This is a spring willow, that is one which flowers before the leaves come. (The summer willows, such as the crack willow, which is often pollarded and found along the margins of streams, flower late.) There are also a lot of silver birch and if you look carefully you can find oak, mountain ash, holly, hazel, hawthorn, ash and sycamore. At the end of the ride you come out on to a forest road. Turn right and in 20 yards, at the junction where there is a lime tree on the corner, turn left. In 20 yards you are standing on another old railway track. Turn left along the grassed-over track.

You are now walking along the Severn and Wye Railway Company's Mineral Loop Line. This was opened in 1872 and was in use for 81 years. It was seven miles long and served many collieries in this part of the forest. All the plants growing on the track have seeded themselves and grown in less than 30 years. It does not take long for nature to cover over the efforts of man. How many flowers can you recognize? Here are some: birds-eye speedwell, wood spurge, horsetail, vetch, clover, stitchwort, heather and the bush guelder rose. There are also clumps of gorse, some of which are sure to be showing some flower whatever the time of year – giving rise to a very sensible old country saying, 'When gorse is in bloom, 'tis kissing time.'

Keep to the old railway track until the path suddenly dives down the embankment to the left. This was where an extension of the Central Line was to pass under the Mineral Loop. It was never completed. Climb back on to the track. The next bridge was built over a forest ride. Go to the far end of the parapet on the right and down the steps to the ride. Turn right under the bridge. At the roadway in 200 yards turn left. In 100 yards, at the junction, turn right along a grass track. You can often see dragonflies along here in summer. As you rise up the bank ahead you suddenly find Speech House lake in front. This was built by the Forestry Commission in 1975 as a conservation lake for wildlife. Pass either side to the other end. Continue a little further and you will come out on to a wide forest road. This is called Spruce Drive, from its fine avenue set out at the beginning of this century. Turn left along the avenue. As you get to the top of the first rise look back and you get a fine view of Staple Edge Hill. Continue through the car park out to the main road. It is the same road you crossed at New Fancy, so you may find people speeding here also. Turn right along the grass verge.

At the crossroads is Speech House. As a royal forest the Forest of Dean had officers to administer it. All that remain now are the Verderers, those responsible for 'all growing and living things', the vert and the venison. The Court of Verderers, often called 'The Court of Speech', was transferred to a new house during the reign of Charles II, which soon became known as Speech House. The Court still sits four times a year, as it did in the time of King Canute, but there is now little or nothing for it to do.

From Speech House cross the triangle of grass at the road junction and go down a grass path which starts in front of the lower 'give way' sign. Now follow the yellow arrows. The trees here are the oldest in the forest. The holly trees are thought to date from the early 17th century, and the oaks from the last years of that century. Th.. y and the beech are long past their prime and have been dying for many years. At the track turn left and so into Russell's Inclosure. In $\frac{1}{4}$ mile, soon after where the Speech House trail crosses from right to left, turn right at a 'T' junction. In another $\frac{1}{4}$ mile, at the end of the ridge, turn right again. As you go down the hill look across the valley to the cranes which stand out on the skyline. These are working in Bixhead Quarry, where the stone comes from for the stone works you saw earlier. Cross over a forest road and at the 'T' junction turn left. Notice that the roadway is surfaced with burnt limestone. Continue to the lowest part of the road, which is in a small wood, and look on the right for a stile with a red arrow. This is the way back.

Just beyond the stile turn right and in a few yards look in the bank on the left. Here a thin coal seam comes to the surface. It is too thin to be of any commercial value. Return to the path and as you go along through the oak wood, if you look carefully, you can see other outcrops of coal in the banks of the stream. Some of these have been worked by the Free Miners. After winding through the trees you come out at the picnic site where you started.

As you drive back to the main road look on the left and you will see where a branch line went off in a gentle curve. It went to the wood distillation works where they produced charcoal for gunpowder, lamp black, naphtha and many other products. It was on the level ground near the crossroads. Opposite the entrance to the roadway you are on, there is a low wall which is all that is left of a 17th-century furnace.

Walk 12   Staunton

5 miles (8 km)

OS sheet 162*

The village of Staunton is set high on the rim of the Forest of Dean, on the A4136 between Monmouth and Coleford. The walk is through the forest and visits one of the well-known viewpoints.

The walk starts from a large layby off the main road, $\frac{1}{2}$ mile out of Staunton on the way to Coleford.

Leave the layby and walk along the road towards Staunton. Just before reaching the end of the woods, turn left on to a forest road, which soon curves left and comes back parallel to the road. Keep straight ahead at the first junction. You will come down the forest road on the right at the end of the walk. In $\frac{1}{4}$ mile turn right at the cross-track. As you go along, pass the turning to the left and when you come to the meeting of four ways bear right up the hill. Again pass a turning on the right and take the next fork right a little further on. At the top of the hill go to the left along a wide forest road. In 50 yards bear right down a pleasant grass track. Go straight over the cross-tracks in 200 yards and soon after the path turns round to the right. In a few yards the track forks. Take the right-hand path, which curves back round the hillside and goes down to a larger track. Walk on down here until you reach a lane.

Keep the same direction along the lane for 50 yards and then turn back on to the lower lane. In $\frac{1}{4}$ mile there is an entrance to the forest on the right. Go in here and take the lower forest road on the left, which goes down the valley. In a further $\frac{1}{4}$ mile you will start to curve round to the right. If you look to the left, at the opposite side of the lane below, at a point just before it reaches a 'T' junction, you will see grass and bushes. It was here that there stood one of the earliest furnaces for smelting iron. It used the new-fangled water power, developed in the early 17th century. Curving round, just above where the furnace stood, is the embankment of a railway which was closed down during the Great War after it had been working for 100 years. It started as the Monmouth Tramroad. The track was made up of short 'L' shaped plates and the wheels of the horse-drawn trucks had no flanges. It was not until 1883 that it was converted into a standard gauge railway, much to the satisfaction of the people of Coleford at the eastern end of the line, who are said to have celebrated the event with great gusto.

The path now goes along the side of the valley for $\frac{1}{4}$ mile following the line of the railway, to where a grass track forks up to the right.

SHEEP   DEER   BADGER   FOX   DOG

Bear right and climb for 50 yards to where a number of tracks branch out. Follow the yellow arrows if you can find them, if not bear slightly left on the most used path which goes up the valley, with the stream on the right. Climb steadily for nearly ½ mile to a junction with a wider grass track. Keep straight ahead to the narrow path in front. Just as you enter the wood to follow this path look about at the sides of the path. There are signs of small animals having their own cross-tracks here. Tracks of fox, badger and deer can all be found, especially if the weather has been wet and the ground is soft.

The badger is a nocturnal animal, so you will not see one going about its business. They do not like people walking about the entrance to their homes. So if you come across a badger 'set' as their house is called, respect their feelings and do not go too close. The deer is elusive. It will have heard or smelt you coming along before you arrive and will have moved off. The fox, too, is mainly nocturnal but may be seen early and late in the day in winter. If we do not see these animals we know where they have been by their footprints, their droppings and other signs left behind. If you know what to look for, places like this show how busy the forest is when we humans are not about.

Continue climbing, rather more steeply now, to cross straight over a ride, still following the yellow arrows. After a further gentle climb bear right up a path which is just inside the wood. You can see a field beyond the hedge and in the distance Beaulieu Wood. Soon the trees stop but keep to the left for 50 yards and then turn back up to the right along a track which eventually curves round to the left between walled banks. Go up here, through a gate and on to a stone track. Turn left and at the end of the hedge on the left, turn left. You will see a yellow arrow on an electricity pole and then more up the hillside on rocks, so follow them to the Buck Stone. This used to be a rocking stone. In 1885 some touring actors came up from Monmouth and pushed too hard. It rolled down towards the road below! With unusual magnanimity the Crown brought it back and cemented it in position.

Away to your right as you climbed the last slope, you could see the village of Staunton through which you will go later. The name Staunton comes from the Anglo-Saxon Stan: a stone or rock. And

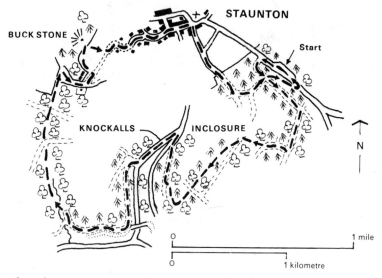

where better to see rocks than near Staunton? They range from the small white pebbles in the quartz conglomerate or pudding stone, to the mysterious standing stones, one of which you pass near the end of the walk. The most notable are the Longstone and the Suck Stone visited on Walk 14. To early man stones must have played an important part in life. Those that have survived the last 4000 years of agricultural activity are but the residue of a complicated network of trackways, mounds, camps, leys and many other so far unexplained physical features.

Return to the signpost and turn towards Christchurch. Follow the yellow arrows. This will take you down to the main street in Staunton. At the village store and post office, which used to be the Royal Oak, bear right along the old village street. Walk up the village street to the old cross opposite the church and turn right. The cottages here were once alms-houses. Go down this ancient walled track to Highmeadow. The field on the left is thought to be the site of a windmill, and the field on the right the site of the manor house, both long since gone. Continue up the hill and just over the rise turn left. Walk down the hill to where the forest road turns round to the left; this is where you came at the beginning of the walk. Go straight over into the wood on a narrow path, still following the yellow arrows. At the main road cross to the footpath and turn left, ignoring the arrows which direct you into the wood. You will see the Longstone standing on the grass verge. The car is 200 yards ahead.

44

Walk 13   Monmouth

7 miles (11 km)

OS sheet 162*

This walk starts out along the banks of the Wye and returns over the hill from which there are fine views over Monmouth and into the mountains of Wales.

Monmouth derives its name from its position at the mouth of the river Monnow which rises in the Brecon Beacons and ends when it runs into the Wye. Surrounded on three sides by rivers, Monmouth lends itself to being a fortified town. There was a river-crossing here in Roman times and probably before that. The town grew when the castle was built and some degree of security was established. Harry of Monmouth, who later became Henry V was born here. By the Act of Union of 1536 Wales was incorporated into England. The March, a district stretching from Glamorgan to Flint and including parts of Herefordshire and Shropshire, was divided up into five shires, one of which was Monmouthshire. This ended two and a half centuries of administrative chaos. Today the county is called Gwent and the administration has moved further west to Cwmbran. An excellent local guide book will provide background information on the town and its surrounding district.

Cars can be parked at various points in the town. The walk starts from the car park near the market, off Bridge Street. This park is signposted a few yards from the famous 13th-century Monnow Bridge. The car park is next to a sports ground with its avenues of trees and the walk starts by crossing this to the far corner near the tennis courts.

Go across the playing fields to the far right-hand corner by the hard tennis courts. In the corner go along an asphalt path at the bottom of the embankment of the A40. Fork left and go over the bridge, down the other side and then turn right under the bridge. Continue up the road past the old railway station (Monmouth, Troy) and turn left along the main road towards Mitchel Troy. In 100 yards, on the sharp right-hand bend, turn left down a lane. Follow the lane past the Troy House and go straight ahead through a bay in a Dutch barn to a gate. Five yards ahead there is another gate and in a further ten yards turn left round the end of the farm buildings. Follow the stone track along the hillside for $\frac{1}{4}$ mile to a sharp left-hand bend where there is a gate. Here you may still be able to enjoy one of the best examples of the binder-twine age which has replaced the iron age on many farms. The highly coloured hinges add a touch of gaiety to the countryside and

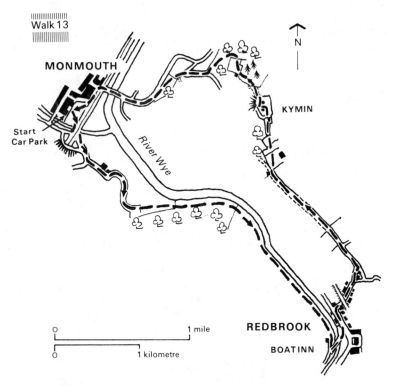

MONMOUTH

KYMIN

Start
Car Park

River Wye

REDBROOK

BOAT INN

N

0   1 mile

0   1 kilometre

the Gordian knot, which does service for a latch, whiles away the
lonely hours for the wayfarer. In a few yards go over a stile to the left of
another gate. Go on up the track and at the next right-hand bend,
where there is a good view over the valley, leave the track and go
straight ahead across the field to the far right-hand corner. Here there
is another gate, 50 yards up from the river, into a wood. Walk through
the wood following the well-trodden path and then along the
meadows for $1\frac{1}{2}$ miles. Dragonflies are numerous here. The bright
blue one with the blue band across its wings is a Damsel fly. They do
nothing but good, for most of their diet consists of mosquitoes and
other small insects.

At the Boat Inn there are waterfalls at the back of the garden. The
cliffs are a part of the old red sandstone block which stretches away to
the west. A few yards past the inn, turn left on to the metal bridge and
cross the river. Go out to the main A466 road to Redbrook and turn
left. Walk along the road past the Wye Valley Garage and Café. In
200 yards, at the Bush Inn, turn right along the road to Coleford.

Go under the bridge with the steeply inclined top which once
carried a tramway and keep to the right-hand side of the road, facing
the oncoming traffic. In 200 yards bear left through a gate and go up a

track at the back of a white house. As you go up look over to the right at the remains of stone buildings. Here was once a 17th-century furnace, a stamping mill and a foundry – what a noisy, dirty place it must have been. Redbrook was once one of the great industrial centres on the edge of the forest. Many a manhole cover in the west of England carries the name of a village in the Forest of Dean.

When the track bears left, keep straight ahead across a small grass triangle to a wooden gate at the side of a white cottage called Sunny Bank. In the sunken track beyond, turn left. You are now following the white arrows of the Offa's Dyke Path. In a few yards you come out on the track again which you keep to as far as the entrance to a farm on the right. Now bear left up the sunken track and continue for $\frac{1}{2}$ mile, passing an old stone barn on the left. A few yards past the barn go over a stile on the right into a field. Turn left towards a stile marked with the white arrow and acorn – the sign for the Offa's Dyke Path. Keep to this path up the hill to the National Trust car park at Kymin.

The first building you come to is the Naval Temple which was erected in 1800 to perpetuate the names of sixteen distinguished admirals whose names are displayed round the walls. The second building, 100 yards further on, was erected in 1794 as a summer house for 'the first gentlemen in Monmouth'. This building, now called the Round House, was where Nelson was entertained to breakfast on the occasion of his visit to Monmouth. In those days 'breakfast' was a substantial meal, eaten about 10.30 a.m., surviving today as the 'workmans' breakfast. From here there is a fine view over Monmouth to the mountains of Mid Wales. A leaflet can be had from the dispenser on the wall of the Round House.

Walk on under the trees to about 20 yards from a stile in the hedge in front. At this point look to the left for a wooden Offa's Dyke sign and turn left on to a narrow path. In five yards turn right down steps and follow the sunken track on down for 100 yards. Keep a lookout on the right for a stile, high on the bank behind a tree. Go over this stile and turn left down through a wood. At the end of the wood go over two stiles into a field. Bear right across the field and curve round to a stile into a wood. Just inside the wood turn left and follow the main path, which is well trodden, down to a lane. Walk on down the lane and in 300 yards, at a sharp right-hand bend, go straight ahead through a metal gate. Keep the same direction to another metal gate into a wood. Here there is a wide path down to the main road. It is best to cross the road before reaching the bend. In 200 yards you can see a wood yard down on the right. This was the site of the other station at Monmouth (May Hill) which was quite extensive. Cross the bridge to the traffic lights and turn right down to the subway. This will take you to the opposite side of the A40. Cross over the side road which leads to the town centre and walk by the side of the school wall, with the A40 on the left. This path will take you to the sports ground where the walk began. In the corner by which you enter the park somebody has had a good idea for a children's playground.

Walk 14   Biblins

6 miles (9.5 km)

OS sheet 162*

Biblins car park has been cut in the hillside, deep in the woods, $\frac{1}{4}$ mile west of the B4432 road between Symonds Yat East and Christchurch. It is signposted with a Forestry Commission notice board at the entrance to a gravel track, one mile south of Yat Rock and $\frac{1}{2}$ mile north of Ready Penny car park, which is on the outskirts of Christchurch.

Leave the car park by the lower left-hand corner, going under the pole across the forest road. Turn left immediately to go down a well-worn path. In 50 yards bear round to the right, ignoring a smaller path which goes straight on. When you get to the top of the next rise keep straight ahead along a wide forest road. At the first right-hand bend bear left up a rutted grass track. On reaching the macadam road turn left and in 100 yards you come to a 'T' junction. Here turn right past two cottages towards the entrance to Bracelands Camp. Just before reaching the entrance bear left and go down a stone track. At the first right-hand bend keep straight ahead down a grassy road which rejoins the stone track as it goes down the hill. At the cross-tracks in the valley go straight across, over a little stream, and start a steady climb of 250 feet up to Staunton church.

When you reach the main road at Staunton, rest for a moment and admire the old barn across the road. The small opening high up the the gable end, which in this case is triangular, was put there to allow owls to get in and out when the barn was full of unthrashed corn. Owls were very welcome, particularly before cats became so plentiful, as they kept the mouse and bird populations down. Cross the road with care and keep to the left of the stump of the old village cross. You are going along what used to be the only road through the village. What is now the main road sweeps round past the churchyard. About 150 years ago it was 'The Great Staunton Bypass' – built by the Turnpike Trust to avoid the narrow streets of the village. How the shopkeepers and innkeepers must have complained. But today the narrow street is best, so go on past the old school, which is on the right. Where did they get the three wonderful stone lintels for the porch? A little further down is a well-proportioned house which has a flight of stone steps on one side leading up to a barn. This is a reminder that much of the land round Staunton, which is now woodland, was once farmland. This was one of the few rural villages in western Gloucestershire. Continue

48

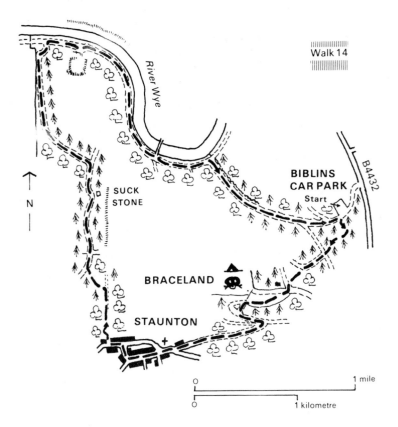

River Wye

BIBLINS
CAR PARK
Start

B4432

N

SUCK
STONE

BRACELAND

STAUNTON

0   1 mile

0   1 kilometre

as far as the post office, which used to be an inn, and bear right. At the main road, again turn left past the White Horse Inn.

Continue along the main road towards Monmouth for 200 yards. Opposite the road sign for a sharp left-hand bend, look for a narrow opening between a house and a wall, marked with a yellow arrow. Go along this path and in $\frac{1}{4}$ mile, after a level path through the wood, follow the yellow arrows which direct you down a path to the left. On reaching a forest road turn right and follow it for $\frac{1}{2}$ mile until the Suck Stone comes into view. This huge lump of rock is said to be the largest boulder in Britain. This rock broke off the cliff above. Looking up you will see the line of the hard rock high above the forest road you have just come along. These rocks dip down away from you at about 40 degrees and so you are looking at the underside of the layer. The rock of the hillside on which you are standing is of a clay formation and is much softer, so it wears away leaving the hard rock unsupported. This eventually fractures and great lumps roll down the hillside. Fortunately for you it does not happen very often.

49

Keep to the forest road past the Suck Stone leaving the yellow arrows to go up the hillside. In $\frac{1}{4}$ mile the track forks. Follow the main track to the left down the hill. In $\frac{3}{4}$ mile, at the bottom of the hill, there is a 'T' junction with an old stone roadway. Here turn right. As you go along you will see through the trees on the left the river Wye. Soon there is a clearing with signs of an old quarry wall. An opening at the far end leads into Hardrock Quarry. Do not go near the rock face as pieces higher up often get dislodged. It shows how the bottom layer of carboniferous limestone has been pushed up on the edge of the forest.

Continue along the roadway and in about 20 yards look on the left for a little opening. Here you have a choice of routes. One is along a narrow path by the side of the river, the other is to continue along the roadway. The path to the left starts by crossing the old Ross–Monmouth railway track, said in its day to be the most beautiful line in England. It then goes down to the waters edge and the narrow path is, for some distance, only a few feet from the water. Go along either route for $\frac{3}{4}$ mile as far as the footbridge over the river. It is an interesting experience to cross the bridge and there are some fine views of the river and the surrounding cliffs from the advantage of height.

Return to the walk upstream, either on the roadway or on the cinders of the railway track. In $\frac{1}{4}$ mile, at the end of the second valley on the right, stop and prepare to walk up the long road to the car. At this point the river, which is now running over an uneven bed of rock, leaves the calm of deeper water. Turn right up the valley and look for the white arrows on the left. If you see them you are in the correct valley. This part of the wood is called The Slaughter, not a name commemorating some terrible battle but a corruption of 'slough' – a wet place. Follow either the path on the left of the stream or the main roadway up the hill. It is a steady climb of nearly 500 feet for a distance of one mile. Keep to the main roadway, ignoring the white arrows when they point to the right. This is the forest road which goes to the corner of the car park.

6½ miles (10·5 km)

OS sheet 162*

This walk starts high on the rim of the forest and goes down to the Wye. The return through the woods involves climbing about 1000 feet, though the gradients are gentle and in some cases steps are provided.

Edge End Forestry Commission car park and picnic site is off the A4136 Monmouth–Gloucestershire road, two miles north of Coleford. The entrance has only a small notice on the road, which says 'Car Park and Bed and Breakfast'. There is a Forestry Commission notice on either side some way along the main road.

The view from the car park is across the valley to English Bisknor.

Leave the car park along the exit road, which is marked with a small blue road sign, and in 20 yards turn left into the wood. You will see yellow arrows painted on the trees, so follow these for the next 1½ miles. At the end of the wood cross the road and go straight ahead. You are now walking with a bank on the left. This is a parish boundary. In the days when the parish as a unit was important, it was necessary to make sure the boundary was known. 1000 years ago there may not have been any permanent identifiable feature just here. Hence the ditch – now filled in – and the bank. The view to the left from the wide grass track is to Hay Bluff and the Black Mountains. After descending for ¼ mile you come to the end of a level forest road. From here there is an excellent view over Lydbrook valley. You will come down through the woods on the side of the hill on the left and go round the two conical mounds, which can just be seen in the valley a mile away in front. They are the waste tips of the Waterloo Mine, 1841–1959, which had to be closed when the workings were flooded. No miners were lost but all the horses perished.

To continue, go to a stile at the end of the forest road and down through the trees. When you get down to a lane with a few houses along it, turn left. This lane gradually deteriorates and when it becomes a path, look on the left in the roots of the trees and you will see an old wall. Spare a thought for the men who must have toiled here. Did they live in the ruined houses you pass as you go along? At the fence go down to the widest stile in this part of the world. In the rough field on the hillside, the stile is in the bottom right-hand corner. Continue just above the hedge until it ends and then bear right to a stile in a wall. Keep the same direction to the road.

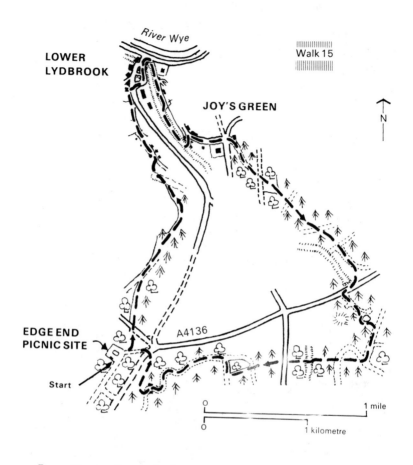

River Wye

LOWER
LYDBROOK

JOY'S GREEN

N

EDGE END
PICNIC SITE

A4136

Start

0   1 mile

0   1 kilometre

Opposite the footpath sign there used to be a tinplate works, founded in the 18th century. Cross the road and turn left. In a few yards turn right down a narrow road which goes past some almost completely demolished cottages on the right. As you go along this quiet road it is difficult to visualize what it was like 100, 200 or even 300 years ago when it was a busy ironworking town. Opposite the Forge Hammer Inn was the Lower Lydbrook forge, built in 1611, one of the first to use waterpower to blow the bellows which increased the airflow to the charcoal, thereby increasing output many times. Continue to the B4228 Ross–Coleford road. Just across the road was a wharf where much of the iron was shipped in small boats down to Monmouth and Chepstow and up into Herefordshire.

At the end of the curved wall overlooking the road junction look for the beginning of a flight of stone steps. These lead up the hillside above the inn. Go up these and at the top look down to the right. Here the railway, which had started as a tramway in 1810, crossed the valley on a viaduct which was built in 1874 at a cost of £7396! Walk along the lower road overlooking the old railway. This road used to continue for $\frac{1}{2}$ mile. It has become so overgrown for most of its length that the only route left is along the railway. Continue along the railway track until the last part of the road, which serves a house on the left, comes down to the railway. Turn left here to go up another flight of steps. They start next to a small cottage. At the top, on the lane, turn right. Just past the end of the garden of the last house on the left, opposite a short stone wall, look in the bank on the left. Here you can see clinker still attached to part of the brickwork which is the remains of a lime kiln. The quarry is just behind. Continue up to the road, passing another kiln next to the road, and so up to the main road at Joy's Green.

Cross the road and bear right up a track into the woods. In $\frac{1}{4}$ mile cross a lane and continue ahead into an oak wood. Follow the main path for 50 yards and then bear right. In 200 yards go over a stile into the forest. 100 yards inside cross straight over another footpath. Go on until you come to a clearing with a cross-path. Cross straight over to go downhill. In $\frac{1}{4}$ mile, at the bottom of the hill there is another clearing and a cross-path. Again cross straight over. As you start to walk towards the path ahead look at the pines on the left. Here you see the result of one of the forest pests. At a height of about 12 feet, four of the Scots pines suddenly become distorted. (You can tell which year it was by counting the whorls or the sections of yearly growth, counting down from the top.) This is the result of the pine shoot moth laying eggs in the centre bud and the larvae eating the inside of the bud. The result is that one or two sides buds have to take over, sometimes producing what is called the 'posthorn' deformation. There is a better example of this by the side of the path in 100 yards.

Walk along this path making sure that children do not stray, especially for the first 30 yards, as the path is on a high bridge over the Greathough Brook. In nearly $\frac{1}{4}$ mile the railway went into a deep cutting before entering a tunnel. This has been filled in recently. Bear right across this area to the main road. Turn right along the grass verge as far as the Waterloo Screens car park. Cross the road and go into the car park. The two conical mounds are just to your right. Pass the first turning on the right and in a few yards bear right on to a coal dust path. This takes you to a small lake.

Go round the lake to the right. On the far side you will come to two planks over a stream. Continue for five yards further and turn right on a path cut through the trees. At the forest road turn right. In about 100 yards turn right along another forest road. In a further $\frac{1}{4}$ mile, when you pass under electricity cables, turn right. Keep to the left of the metal poles. In 200 yards, at the end of the clearing, seek the path under a chestnut tree and go down to the railway. At the top of the far embankment keep the same direction and go out to the road – which you will come upon suddenly. Cross straight over, with care, to a grass path through the trees. At the forest road go straight ahead uphill. You are now in Swallowvallets Inclosure. Continue for $\frac{1}{4}$ mile and after the path has levelled out, at a 'T' junction with a wide grass road, turn right. In 200 yards turn left on to a forest road. After the stile at the side of the barrier, the forest road curves round the head of Cannop valley for $\frac{3}{4}$ mile. On rounding one of the many bends you come upon the Brook Coalmine No 2. This is a Free Miners' mine. Men of Dean Forest have ancient rights to mine for iron and coal in the forest. They are allowed gales or areas in the forest, and this is one.

Continue round the bend and fork right following the red arrows of a forest trail. In 100 yards turn right to come to the main road. Cross with great care and then bear left to the exit road from the car park. Walk along the gravel road back to the car.

Walk 16

Pope's Hill ✓

$4\frac{1}{2}$ miles (7 km)

OS sheet 162*

This is a walk in the less frequented part of the Forest of Dean, where there are some small wooded hills. Pope's Hill is $1\frac{1}{2}$ miles east of Cinderford. It is signposted $\frac{1}{2}$ mile from the village of Littledean on the road to Gloucester.

From the highest point of the common at Pope's Hill there is a magnificient view of the upper tidal reaches of the river Severn. It is in this part of the river that the Severn Bore starts to build up. The Heart of England Tourist Board produces an excellent information sheet with calendar, so that you can tell when and where to see this unusual sight. It is well worth seeing. Pope's Hill was an important place in the early industrial history of Dean. Before the development of water power to work the bellows in the 16th century, iron furnaces were built on the tops of the hills so as to make use of all the wind there was. It is difficult to imagine the smoke and fumes of a windy day where there is now only the pure air of the Severn estuary.

Cars can be parked just clear of the wood near the 'T' junction at the end of the village nearest the wooded hill. The walk starts from here.

Standing at the 'T' junction facing the wooded hill, go to the left of the house in front and up a grass track. This climbs up behind the house. At the top of the first rise keep straight ahead, leaving the small enclosure belonging to the waterboard on your left. At the junction bear right down the hill. At the first stony track cross straight over to go down and merge with a stony road.

At the main road in $\frac{1}{4}$ mile go straight over and in five yards turn right along a slightly sunken track. In 100 yards, just past a small moss-covered boulder on the right, fork left and take the path into the wood. In another 100 yards, where the path starts to go downhill, fork left on to a less defined path going up under the trees. After a few yards look about as you climb the hill. It is just possible to see the level platforms made by the charcoal burners as a base for their 'pits'. After a while, where the path levels out for a short distance, there is a level round platform about five yards across. They have not been used for many years so in summer they are difficult to see but in winter they can be detected dotted about all over this hillside. In a survey of Dean Forest in the 13th century there recorded over 2000 such platforms.

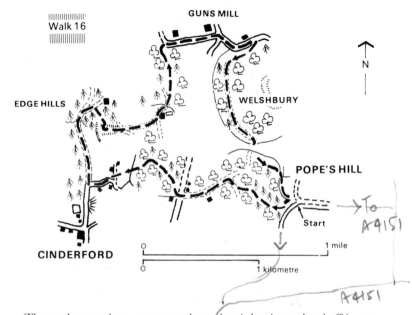

GUNS MILL

EDGE HILLS

WELSHBURY

POPE'S HILL

To
A4151

Start

CINDERFORD

0   1 mile

0   1 kilometre

A4151

    The path now rises more steeply and as it begins to level off it goes
over another pit. How many can you see as you go through the wood?
When you come to a view over the valley down to the right, take the
right fork. In a further 50 yards, at the end of the trees, bear left across
open land towards a house on the skyline. Join the lane which goes
past the house and on up to a sharp left-hand bend with a forest road
on the right. The walk goes along this track to the right but for an
excellent view over the Severn valley walk 100 yards to the left along
the lane. To continue the walk return to the sharp bend.

    Go along the forest road which is round the head of the valley. A few
yards after crossing a brook and passing three old pines, fork right
down a track into a larch plantation. When a house comes into view in
front look on the right for a grass track which goes back along the
hillside below you. Go down this and when you come to the edge of the
gully, turn left and zigzag down to derelict quarry buildings. At the
bottom turn left down the valley, following the stream. Notice how
well the culvert on the left carrying the stream was made, many years
ago.

    Continue down the valley for $\frac{1}{4}$ mile to a stone building which is now
a pumping house, pushing water up to a reservoir near where you
looked over the Severn valley. Turn left on a track to a gate and then
fork right – either just below or just after the gate. Follow the track
downhill for $\frac{1}{4}$ mile. On entering an old woodland, bear slightly right
to the road where three streams meet. Turn right and go down the
lane. At the bottom of the lane there is a farm on the left. This used to

be Guns Mill. When it was first built is not known but in 1683 it was being rebuilt and the present ivy-covered structure is a furnace of that date. It is subject to a Building Preservation Order and has been surveyed by the Gloucestershire Industrial Archaeology Society, but is in danger of collapse unless money is found to make it safe. It is known to have produced almost 780 tones of iron in 1705, when there were also two grist mills and a fulling mill using the water from the mill pond, which alas is now dry. By 1743 it was a paper mill.

Go out to the road and take the lane ahead, signposted Flaxley. In about 300 yards, just past a black and white house on the left, turn right on to a track which goes up the hillside and overlooks Guns Mill. At the first left-hand bend the track becomes a wide forestry road. High on the hill to the left, hidden in the trees, are the well-defined fortifications of a pre-Roman camp called Welshbury. Continue for $\frac{1}{2}$ mile to the end of the wood and then turn right over a stile into a field. The public right of way to the left is impassible so cross the narrow neck of land to the gate opposite and enter the wood. In a few yards turn left and in $\frac{1}{4}$ mile bear left to leave the wood on to a track which runs just below the boundary of the wood. This track takes you to the 'T' junction where you started the walk.

Walk 17   Symonds Yat East

6 miles (9.5 km)

OS sheet 162*

Symonds Yat is a famous beauty spot five miles south of Ross on Wye and three miles north of Coleford. The walk starts from the Yat Rock car park, which is above Symonds Yat East, (not to be confused with Symonds Yat West, which is on the opposite side of the river).

From the A40, Ross (M50) to Monmouth road, take the B4229 road to Goodrich and in ¾ mile turn right to cross a narrow metal bridge. From Coleford follow the B4432 road. Symonds Yat is well signposted from all directions.

Yat is an old local term for a gateway and Symonds comes from a high Sheriff of Herefordshire who owned much land hereabouts in the 17th century.

The walk starts from a small car park next to the main road, on a bend 200 yards from the wooden footbridge over the road at the top of the hill. If this car park is full, the entrance to the main car park and coach park is 200 yards nearer to Coleford and the entrance roadway goes down and round behind the trees on the opposite side of the road to the small car park. If you use the main park, walk out through the exit and the small park is a few yards to the right across the road.

Leave the small car park along a path which starts opposite the entrance. This is an attractive walk, laid out by the Forestry Commission, along the top of the Coldwell Rocks. In ¼ mile there is a large and very solid stile and beyond it the path winds round the top of a number of narrow valleys, keeping almost level. In a further ½ mile there is a fork in the path. The one to the left goes downhill, that to the right goes up to a stile, which can be seen from the fork. Bear right to the stile and in the field beyond go straight ahead. As you come to the top of the rise bear right towards a small stile in a wooden fence, 50 yards to the left of the farm buildings. From here cross straight over a narrow field to the corner of a hedge where there is a sign indicating English Bicknor. The church on the hill opposite is at English Bicknor. Continue down to the lane and turn left.

As you go down the lane you pass the drive to the house called Rosemary Topping on the left. This is also the name given to the small round hill which forms the end of the ridge. At the bottom of the hill the road turns into a track as it passes the last cottage, eventually coming to a gate and stile. Keep to the track as it goes along the bottom of a field with a wood on the right. When the wood ends there

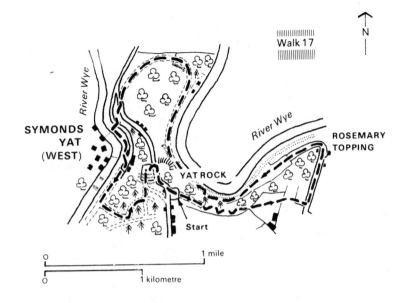

SYMONDS YAT (WEST)

River Wye

River Wye

ROSEMARY TOPPING

YAT ROCK

Start

0   1 mile

0   1 kilometre

is a fine view of the Wye down below on the right. In the wood on the other side of the river is the drowned boy's memorial stone seen on Walk 21. Follow the track across the field down to a wood. When the track sweeps round to the right to a derelict barn, keep straight ahead through the wood, next to a fence on the right. At the end of the fence the track turns right on to an old railway embankment. Here turn left.

As you walk along the old railway track you come to a gate. According to the map you are 100 yards from the small car park at the start of the walk – but it is also 300 feet above you.

Continue past the bricked-up entrance to the railway tunnel and soon start climbing up a forest road. In about $\frac{1}{4}$ mile there are some rough stone steps on the left. These would take you to the road just below the Yat Rock. The continuation of this path on the right of the forest road takes you down steps to a riverside walk. If this is followed it involves a very steep ascent of some 200 feet at the end of a wood, to bring you back to the forest road. Otherwise continue along the forest road rising gently. Just past a bend, in about $\frac{1}{2}$ mile, there is an excellent example on the left of Nature's cement, the conglomerate rock. This has lasted some 100,000,000 times longer than man's equivalent. Just past here you come to double gates. Those who went down along the riverside walk will toil up some slippery steps to this point. Walk on for another $\frac{1}{2}$ mile round the north side of Huntsham Hill to the road up to Yat Rock.

Cross the narrow road and walk uphill for 50 yards to a small passing place for cars on the right. In the middle of this passing place bear right down a path through the bushes. The start of this path may be difficult to see from the road but once inside the wood there is a clear way down to the lane to Symonds Yat East. On the lane, turn left for 20 yards and then follow a grass track across the field on the right.

At the riverside you may find a ferry working which would take you over to the Old Fleece Inn. If you cross you may like to continue downstream for nearly $\frac{1}{2}$ mile and re-cross the river by another ferry. If you do not wish to go over the river, turn left along the riverside path to the Saracen's Head, where the lower ferry operates.

Continue along the side of the river past the hotels which cater for fishermen during the salmon season. Beyond the last hotel there is a choice of three parallel routes – the old road under the cliffs, the rough path next to the river and the old railway track between the two. The river at this point has many small rapids, which in this case is the result of the island (a fallen block of lower dolomite which has encouraged silting) speeding up the river flow. It provides an excellent place for innumerable canoeists to learn how to handle their craft. $\frac{1}{4}$ mile from the last hotel there is a path going up a narrow valley to the left. Look for a short flight of stone steps between the railway and the old road, which will tell you where the valley starts. Many years ago there used to be an important ford across the river here.

Go up the path which climbs steadily. When it levels out Yat Rock is reached by bearing left. There are many well-used paths in this part of the wood, as it is near to the car park. Some have the red arrows of a forest trail. All paths to the left or ahead lead to the car and coach park. Join the entrance roadway and go towards the log cabin. At one point you will be able to see how the roadway has been cut through the ridges which formed part of the defences of a prehistoric fort. Pass the log cabin and follow the signs, over the footbridge, to Yat Rock. The small car park, where the walk started, is 200 yards along the road from the footbridge.

Walk 18   Mitcheldean

5½ miles (9 km)

OS sheet 162*

It is to this area that many university and school parties come to study geology. The first part of the walk does a very rapid survey of the main features which can be seen. The outward journey is along the northeastern rim of the basin of carboniferous limestones. It is possible to see rocks which were laid down over a period of some six million years because they have been heaved up to an angle of 70 degrees in later earth movements.

The walk starts from a point ½ mile southwest of Mitcheldean, which is where the B4224 meets the A4136 Gloucester–Monmouth road. In the middle of the village a lane goes up the hill, signposted Drybrook. Drive up here and in ½ mile, on a sharp right-hand bend at the top, turn left and park well clear of the track. The start can also be reached from Drybrook by taking the road from the centre of the town signposted Mitcheldean.

Leave the car and go up an avenue of oak trees on a track which starts between two posts. The main track bears left to Stenders Farm. In ¼ mile a white gate comes into sight leading into a field. You will now be able to see, by the surface of the track, that you are walking over sandstone. This is called Drybrook sandstone after the village of Drybrook a mile away behind you, where there is an enormous quarry. At the top of the hill, follow the track round to the right past some gnarled old beech trees which have been wind-blasted. In 200 yards look over to the right through a gap in the trees to the quarry which stretches all along the hillside. When you reach the lane go straight across if you want to see some of the geology of the district but if not, turn right down the lane to the main road which you cross, and ignore the next paragraph.

Between the lane and the far side of the hill the various layers of limestone rocks come to the surface. In 20 yards bear left next to a garden wall and when it ends bear left again. If this path is overgrown go a little further round, but make your way to the right-hand end of a stone wall. Here, under a fence, is the only exposure of the top layer of limestone. We now go to the far side of the hill to see the other rocks in the order in which they were laid down. Walk on across the first small ridge and go down across a flat platform left by old quarry workings. Continue to the right of a wire garden fence and go round behind Woodland Rise. In 100 yards go down a sunken grass path at the side

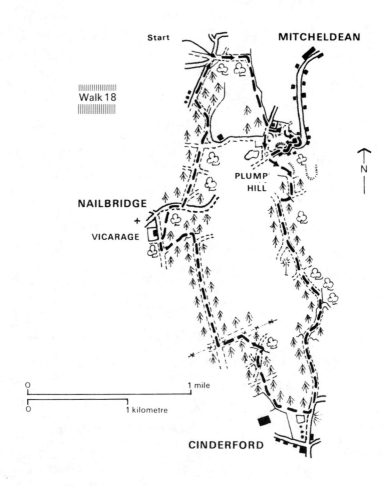

Start

MITCHELDEAN

Walk 18

PLUMP HILL

NAILBRIDGE

VICARAGE

N

0   1 mile

0   1 kilometre

CINDERFORD

of Vention Cottage. You are now on a shelf just above the main road
as it comes up to a large bend. Here there is quartz conglomerate and
nearer the bend Tintern sandstone. Walk on along the pavement and
two yards past the manhole cover (by Herbert Young of Cinderford)
there is an exposure of limestone shale in the bank on the right. Notice
the almost vertical bedding. At the end of the pavement cross the road
and in 100 yards pass a large dolomite quarry. From just past the little
chapel you can see how the rocks dip down steeply to the left. Continue up the road to the second turning on the right where the lane
comes down to the road. Here turn left.

Go into the disused quarry and walk on ahead. At the top of the rise you can look down into a part of an old sandstone quarry. Here you are looking at the tilted-up floor of an ancient river estuary which existed 300,000,000 years ago, much the same as the Severn estuary you can see in the distance. Geologists may now make a further short detour, others should go to a track to the right leading into the wood. Walk along this for 200 yards and turn right, ignoring the next paragraph.

Geologists may care to go round to the right of the sandstone quarry, next to the wood, noticing the continuation of the quarry strata in the bank on the right. On the other side of the ridge is a limestone quarry. Much of this has also been filled in but on the sloping ground below the wood, by searching amongst the rocks, white dolomite crystals and black veins of iron can be seen. To continue the walk, go up to the top corner of the quarry clearing and along a track into the wood. In 100 yards bear left.

Ahead is a wide stile and a path which leads out of the wood and on to a forest road. Turn left and when the electricity wires bear left, follow them. Along this path which is just below the television relay station, the bank on the right is covered with bilberries and at the bottom of the bank an attractive lichen (cladonia), slightly different from the common cup found on Walk 23. At the cross-paths go straight ahead, still following the electricity wires. Half way between the second and third single poles you cross a band of limestone. We can only guess at this by the sudden change of vegetation on the left where there is a mass of travellers' joy climbing up the trees – this is a plant which only grows on limestone. We can prove it a little further on. At the bottom of the slope bear right to a gate and stile on to a stone road. Turn right. As you go round the first right-hand bend, 10 yards past the layby on the left, look at the trees on the right. They are covered with travellers' joy again. Now look at the bank at the side of the roadway and you can see the band of blue-grey limestone which we guessed was there.

Continue along this road until it joins a lane. In 100 yards admire the view to the left. With your back to the view of the river Severn, go between the railings and the wood. As the oak trees thin out there is a fine view over the upper coal measures of the Forest of Dean. At your feet the ground is carpeted with the common grasses of a typical heathland. Bear round to the right and go along a well-used path into the wood with pines on the right. Keep ahead over a forest road and when the path joins a wider track, follow it for 100 yards. At the junction are the remains of a Free Miners' coalmine. The shaft has been concreted over so it is safe to explore. You then fork right. When you come to a gate, go over a stile at the side and turn left, back across the track to take a narrow grass path to the left of the chestnut trees.

At the first cross-path in $\frac{1}{4}$ mile turn left and go downhill under the electricity wires. On reaching a forest road turn right. In $\frac{1}{2}$ mile, when the forest road turns round to the right, go straight ahead down a path. At the bottom of the slope bear left through the trees. You are now at the base of a coal tip from a disused mine further up the valley. In the bed of the small stream is an orange-yellow mud, reminding one that the Forest of Dean used to supply ochres to paint manufacturers. Cross the stream and go to a path down the valley. As you go down, there are signs of an old tramway.

On reaching the cross-tracks turn right. In 100 yards pass an ancient beech tree on the left – what changes this old fellow must have seen. At the beginning of the high wall bear right and follow the yellow arrows. As you go up through the trees, look over to the left at the high prison-like walls surrounding the house. This is a vicarage! At the main road turn right along the grass verge for 100 yards and cross to a gate. From here the yellow arrows go off to the right, but you keep straight ahead, following the electricity wires. At the top of the hill cross over the track and keep in the same direction for 200 yards, to pass under the wires and on to another track. Now turn left and in 100 yards pass No. 4 post on the Wilderness Forest Trail. Follow the main track for $\frac{1}{4}$ mile down to the cottages on a rough lane and turn right. This used to be the main road from Monmouth to Gloucester and in the 13th century was called the Spanneway. It was improved by a turnpike trust in the 17th century but later abandoned. Walk up this old road to the sharp bend where the car is parked.

A bridge near Lodges farm on the old road up to Newlands

A quiet glade
in Haugh Wood

Relaxing on the
Wye above
Symonds Yat

The Monnow Bridge, Monmouth - the last fortified
bridge gateway in Britain

Walk 19   Lea Bailey Inclosure

4 miles (6·5 km)

OS sheet 162

This walk is on a low dome of rock surrounded by hills. It is known to geologists as the Hope Mansel Dome. The centre, where the walk goes, is lower Devonian brownstones, which were folded during the inter-Carboniferous period of earth movement about 300,000,000 years ago. The surrounding hills are edged with quartz conglomerate.

The Lea Bailey Inclosure is near Lane End which is mid-way between Ross and Cinderford. It can be reached either from Lea on the A40 Ross–Gloucester road four miles from Ross, or from Drybrook. From Lea turn on to the Mitcheldean road and in $\frac{1}{2}$ mile turn right for Drybrook. In a further $\frac{1}{2}$ mile there is a 'T' junction; the car park is on the right. From Drybrook, which is two miles north of Cinderford, follow the road past the entrance to the Euroclydon Hotel, through the cutting known as Bailey Gate and down to a turning to Lea on the right. The car park is just past the turning on the right. Drive in under the trees to park.

Leave the car park and cross the side road from Lea, then go on to a path at the side of a bus stop which is 50 yards from the road junction. Follow this path into the wood. In 100 yards it comes to a road bridge over a cutting which is fast disappearing under trees and bushes. This used to be the railway line from Drybrook, the other side of the hill, to Mitcheldean Junction on the GWR. Up on the hills to the left are some of the first iron mines in Dean. They supplied the Roman industrial town of Ariconium, two miles to the north, near Weston under Penyard. A little way up the road to the left is an excellent exposure of quartz conglomerate or pudding stone, a hard concrete-like rock responsible for the ridge of hills round the Forest of Dean. It also forms a ring round most of this walk and is most striking, as it goes for two miles past Ham Grove Farm, away to the right.

Cross the road and go down the track through the oak and beech wood towards Ham Grove Farm. When the wood on the right ends and the fields start, turn right on to a path which comes back into the wood. In a few yards bear left to a gate. This leads to a grass track just inside the wood. In 100 yards turn left and go down just inside the wood with the hedge on the left. At the bottom corner of the wood follow the path round to the right. As you go along you will notice that the path has a good firm base. This is because it used to be a well-used

65

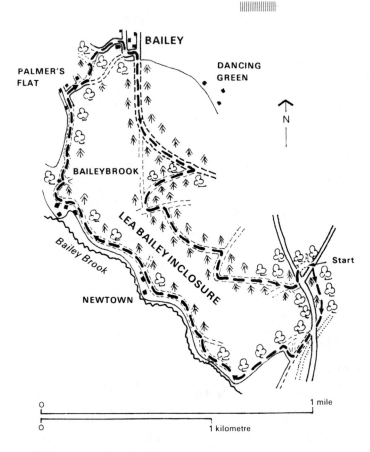

road. It is still marked on maps as Elm Lane and it served the settlement of Newtown which you will come to soon.

On this walk you will come across great clumps of broom, a smooth-leaved shrub up to six feet high, whose yellow flowers are followed by attractive, hairy-edged pods. These pods eventually go black and when ripe twist and eject the seed for some distance – a most entertaining sight. The plant contains an alkaloid and is very dangerous. On no account should children be allowed to eat the seeds. A point in favour of this plant however is that when the stems are bound in bundles they make good sweeping tools – hence the name.

66

When the path reaches a gravel track bear left. You can see the type of rock which underlies the dome opposite the cottage, where there is a small exposure in the bank. A few yards past the cottage the track turns right up the hill or bears left. This is the centre of Newtown! Up to the right is Lawer's Bath Spring. Deep inside the hill the rock is saturated with water and this comes out at various points round the dome. At each point a group of houses will be found, many of which are now derelict. This is a reminder that until very recent times man was only able to live where he could find a natural supply of water.

Continue along the track to the left around the edge of the inclosure. Pass round behind another cottage. This settlement was called Baileybrook, named after the stream you have been following for the last mile. When the track rises up to a junction of five ways, bear left along a track which rises gently. In $\frac{1}{4}$ mile pass a cottage on the left and join a macadam track. In 50 yards turn right on to a lane and follow this for 200 yards, to pass a house below on the left. At this clearing the road bears right and goes up into the wood. Just round the bend bear left along a grass forest road. Follow this round a left-hand bend and in a further 100 yards there is a cross-path. Turn right and go through the trees to a well-used track. To the left this goes down to Palmers Flat; you turn right to Palmers Hill. At the 'T' junction turn right and follow the lane round to the left to another 'T' junction. Here turn right and go over a cattle grid to follow a well-used, metalled, forest road. Over to the left you can see two houses which form part of the settlement called Dancing Green. With Sparrow Corner and Lane End a little further round to the right, this completes the group of eight settlements round the dome.

As the road reaches its highest point there is a grass track on the right leading back along the hillside. Follow this until it reaches a 'T' junction with a stone track. Turn left here and in 200 yards turn right along a grass track. At the next junction turn right and follow the track round the hill to the left. This takes you down to a gate and stile a few yards from the road junction where the car is parked. Bear left across the road to the car park.

Walk 20

Lower Lydbrook

7 miles (11 km)

OS sheet 162*

This walk starts from what used to be called Lydbrook Junction. Now that the railway has disappeared it has lost its name, for the signposts have 'Lydbrook Junction' painted out. On the B4228, Ross–Coleford road between Lydbrook and English Bicknor there is a sharp bend at the bottom of a hill. On the bend is the entrance to Reed Corrugated Cases Ltd. Nearby there is an old section of road which was left when the new road was made at the time the railway bridge was dismantled. This makes an excellent place to park. It is next to the turning to Lydbrook Hospital.

Cross the road and follow the footpath sign to Welsh Bicknor. You are now in Gloucestershire so on the hill behind you is English Bicknor. Across the river is part of south Herefordshire, which used to be subject to Welsh law, so the area is called Welsh Bicknor.

Go down the track at the side of the factory. Continue to the disused railway bridge and go up the bank on the left to cross to the other side of the Wye. The plant growing in the river is water crowfoot. At the end of the bridge go down to the right by the side of the river. Pass the house on the left and follow the path up to the left to the old vicarage, now a youth hostel. Ten yards before reaching the gate marked 'No entry before 5 p.m.', stop.

Turn right and go down the path in front of the hostel. The church on the left was built in 1859 and paid for mostly by the rector. Now follow the path along the side of the river. In ¼ mile you are opposite Lower Lydbrook. Here there is a sudden drop on water level, where the river runs over a hard outcrop of rock. The river is made to run fast against the nearside bank and this is causing the inside of the curve to be worn away. Usually it is the outside bank which is eroded. There is also an island starting to grow in midstream. The group of buildings high up on the left as you walk along belong to the Mill Hill Fathers. It used to be the home of Cardinal Vaughan.

As you go along the meadows you can just see, high up on the opposite hillside, the line of the old tramway from Lydbrook to Bishopswood. Just below Bishopswood, where there is now a collection of chalets, was a wharf called Cinderhill Wharf, from the mountain of cinders left by earlier workers. These were re-used in the furnaces at Lydbrook, so there are none left now. Two furnaces up the

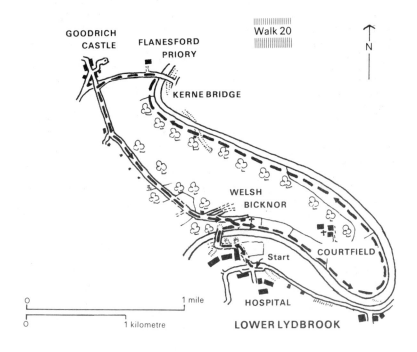

GOODRICH
CASTLE

FLANESFORD
PRIORY

Walk 20

N

KERNE BRIDGE

WELSH
BICKNOR

COURTFIELD

Start

0   1 mile

0   1 kilometre

HOSPITAL

LOWER LYDBROOK

hillside were operating before 1602 and at one time this was a busy part of the river.

Continue by the side of the river through a wood. When you come to a stone wall on the left, you are at the place where the Ross–Monmouth line crossed. It is strange to think that the line did not close until 1965. On emerging from the wood, follow the path to Kerne Bridge. Near here there used to be a ferry and the story is that when Henry IV was here, a messenger arrived who told him of the birth of his son, later Henry V. In great joy the King gave the messenger, whose name was Kerne, the rights of the ferry. There is no record of the comments of the original ferryman.

Go up the steps. Now take great care emerging on to the road. Turn left, keeping close against the hedge until you are on the footpath. In a few yards there is a good view of the farm across the field on the right, which used to be Flanesford Priory. It was founded by Richard Talbot – who came from a notable Midland family – in 1346 when he obtained possession of Goodrich Castle through his wife. It is now Bemor Pottery and Silk Screen Printers. Continue up the road and climb up the path at the side of the bridge.

The entrance to Goodrich Castle is 100 yards down the road on the right. Ye Olde Hostelrie is 100 yards further. This is a romantic inn, with its Gothic windows and pinnacles, built in 1830. Was it copied from an old missal? It is interesting to discover that it was moulded in the same fashion as Goodrich Court, now mercifully demolished, which stood on the next promontory to the castle. When Wordsworth saw it he called it 'an impertinent structure'. On the A40(T) there still stands the gatehouse, complete with machicolated towers and portcullis.

To return, walk up the lane from the road bridge. As you walk along the hillside there are magnificent views down to the river Wye. Keep to the lane over the hill and down the other side through the fields of the Courtfield estate. Keep to the right each time the road forks and go down towards the youth hostel. When you see a sign directing you down a public footpath, go down to the front of the buildings and turn right to the river and the railway bridge. Retrace your steps past the paper factory to the car.

Walk 21

Goodrich Castle ✓

6½ miles (9·5 km)

OS sheet 162*

If you like riverside walking you can do 4½ miles to Welsh Bicknor on this walk and then turn to Walk 20 to continue along the riverside back to Goodrich. This makes a total of 8½ miles, of which seven miles are some of the most beautiful in the Wye Valley.

Goodrich Castle stands high on a promontory overlooking the river Wye, three miles south of Ross on Wye. It is well signposted as an ancient monument on the A40 trunk road and the B4228 south of Ross.

There is an extensive car park and picnic area from which the walk starts.

Leave the car park and go back down the entrance road to the village. In winter, check to see what time the car park closes. There will be a notice hanging at the entrance. Cross straight over the crossroads and bear left to go down the lane with the school on the right. Just beyond these buildings turn right through a small gate and cross the well-mown playing field. In the next field follow the path up the bank to the left-hand corner. Now go across another rough field and into a tidy churchyard. Go round to the south of the church and opposite the porch there is the stump of an old cross, dated 1692. Continue through the churchyard, across a paddock and on to a lane. In 50 yards, at the 'T' junction by the black and white house, turn right. On reaching the Cross Keys Inn, with its attractive little mounting block to make it easier for riders to mount their horses, turn left down a track at the side of a house. Follow the footpath sign. At the farmyard in 100 yards keep to the right and follow the track into a field. Go ahead across the field, passing about 20 yards to the left of the fine oak tree, towards a younger oak at the left-hand end of a wood. Here there is no stile but step over the wire fence and go down to the right following the hedge round the field. On the other side of the hedge is a sewage works, so you may have to hurry. After turning left and then right you will find a stile in the corner of the field. From here you have a good view of both Symonds Yats. 'Yat' means a gate, and Symonds was a 17th-century property owner in the district. Bear left across a field and go down to the left of a house and garden to the road. Walk along the lane opposite, signposted to Symonds Yat East.

At the iron bridge go down to a path to the right of the bridge and

71

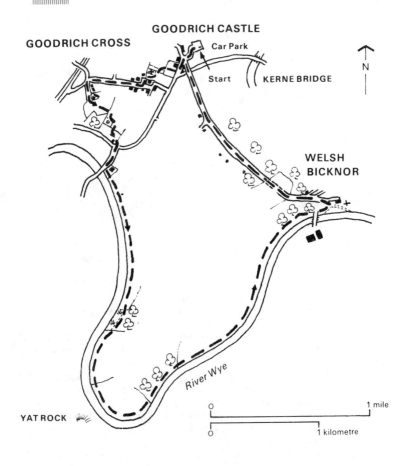

GOODRICH CASTLE

GOODRICH CROSS

Car Park

Start

KERNE BRIDGE

N

WELSH
BICKNOR

River Wye

YAT ROCK

0   1 mile

0   1 kilometre

turn left under the bridge. Now follow the path along the side of the river. On the left is Coppet Hill and here you can see the line where the conglomerate outcrops. The blocks in the river are lumps which have broken off. In ½ mile go through a small wood and then into meadows again. This is the place that people can see when standing at the viewpoint at Yat Rock. If you look up at the top of the rock in front you may see a row of small heads peering down at you. As you go round the bend you will see a number of the rocks standing out of the trees across the river. It is lower dolomite, a type of limestone laid ˙ wn 320 million years ago – for those who would like to know, it has the chemical formula $(Ca\,Mg)\,CO_3$, which tells its own story.

Again enter a wood to find all the trees are covered with travellers' joy, better known in autumn as old man's beard. About 100 yards inside the wood there is a giant sweet chestnut tree on the left, its bark spiralling round the trunk like some gigantic gear wheel. A little further on look for a small railed-off tomb-like memorial on the left. It was erected in 1804 to John Whitehead Warre, when this five-year-old lad drowned in the Wye. '. . . this monument is here erected to warn parents and others, to be careful how they trust this deceitful stream. Particularly to exhort them to learn and observe the directions of the Humane Society for the recovery of persons apparently drowned. Alas it is with extreme sorrow, here commemorated, what anguish is felt from the want of this knowledge . . .'

Continue on through the wood and then through meadows. The wooded hill on the right is called Rosemary Topping. Look out for dragonflies in summer. In $\frac{3}{4}$ mile the path winds through scrub and then along at the bottom of a wood. Pass under the old railway bridge. In 100 yards the path starts to rise up towards the Youth Hostel. Ten yards from the gate marked 'no entry before 5 p.m.' stop. Here you have a choice of routes. To the right along the riverside is four miles – turn to Walk 20 and omit the first two paragraphs. Alternatively to go over the hill ($2\frac{1}{4}$ miles) turn left up a grass path.

For those turning left it is an easy walk along a quiet lane, reached by going up the grass path to the left of the barn. At the top go on along the lane past the entrance to Courtfields Court. This lane goes over the hill and down to Goodrich. Do not miss the fine views of the river Wye, far below on the right.

Walk 22   Welsh Newton

5½ miles (9 km)

OS sheet 162(*)

Welsh Newton lies on the A466, Monmouth–Hereford road, three miles north of Monmouth. The A466 winds in a narrow valley as it leaves Monmouth and the church and a few houses are next to this road. The walk starts from Welsh Newton Common which is ¾ mile away on the hill behind the church. Leave the A466 by the church and take the road up the hill which is signposted Llangarron. In ½ mile, at the top of the hill, turn right to Welsh Newton Common. Continue along the very winding lane for ½ mile and at the fork, with its red telephone box, bear right. In a further 200 yards the County Council has erected a smart bus shelter. Cars may be parked in this part of the common, making sure not to obstruct the access to any of the houses. The walk will start from the bus shelter.

Walk along the stone track opposite the bus shelter and pass the village shop and the water tower on the right. When the track turns right you turn left along a grass track. The view from the gateway on the right is towards Cardiff, with Monmouth hidden behind trees on the left. In a few yards go through the trees and bear left along a track. As you near the end of the track there is a group of beech trees on the left. It was from here, some years ago, before the surrounding hedges and trees had grown so high, that it was possible to see nine counties on a clear day. At the 'T' junction turn right to go past a farm. Continue along the narrow hedged lane for ½ mile. Away to the left is St. Wolstan's Farm with its enormous grain silo, sited on high ground next to the farm.

At the end of the lane bear right along a track between hedges. This used to be a continuation of the lane along the ridgeway and eventually down to Monmouth. In ¼ mile there is a wood on the right and a few yards further on a wood begins on the left. Here turn left and go down just inside the wood. The footpath should be a few yards to the left of the present track, but until it is cleared of the trees, bushes and brambles, keep to the track. In 200 yards the track forks. At this point look to the left for a narrow path through the bushes. Go along this path for a few feet to a gate and from here continue down the hill on the correct line of the footpath, which is a wide hedged grass track. In 200 yards go through a gate into a field and continue with the hedge on the left. Notice how this hedge was built on top of a bank, which might have started life as a stone wall. Was this once an old

74

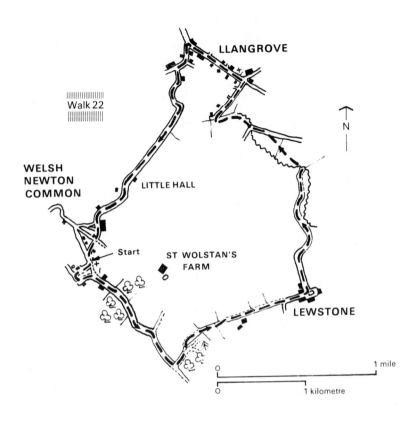

Walk 22

LLANGROVE

WELSH
NEWTON
COMMON

LITTLE HALL

Start

ST WOLSTAN'S
FARM

LEWSTONE

N

0   1 mile

0   1 kilometre

boundary? Pass through a gate and in a further 100 yards go through another gate, so as to walk with the hedge on the right. Go past the house called Great Hillshone and follow the hedge on the right down into Lewstone.

Turn left along the lane marked as a 'no through road' and in ¼ mile pass a house on the left. The lane now becomes a hedged track and goes downhill, to become no more than a footpath at the bottom of the hill. The hedge plants on either side have now grown up into trees or have been stifled and died. Continue up the valley with the brook sometimes close by on the right and sometimes below across a field. The path eventually turns back into a grass way used by the farmer to reach the surrounding fields. On reaching a gate across the track you will see ahead no trace of the hedged road you have been following for nearly a mile. Ordnance Survey maps of the beginning of this century show two hedges going up the hillside in front. How easy it is for the countryside to change and leave no trace of its previous design.

Looking round the hillside we find that many of the hedges round the fields are not more than 200 years old and for a long time before that these parts were subject to Celtic husbandry. Near Lewstone out in the middle of a field, was once found a tesselated pavement – there may be more below the surface of these hills. We also know from aerial photography and archaeological field work that land shortage was becoming a problem as long ago as 500 BC. How many times have these hills known a change of clothing?

From the gate into the field bear left to go half way up the side of the round-topped hill. Go over a stile in a fence and aim for a point half way down the right-hand hedge. The stile is hidden from view by the overhang of a tree. On the lane beyond turn left. In 200 yards when the lane goes round to the left keep straight ahead to a gate. From here the footpath goes towards an old barn with a corrugated iron roof, which can just be seen up the valley. Continue up this valley to the left of a dried-up watercourse as far as the corner. Cross the footbridge and stile on to the end of a track which gradually improves until it comes out on to the main road through Llangrove.

At this point, should you need a rest, you will find a pleasant circular seat under the tree on the corner. Across the road is the 1887 village water supply. Turn left along the road past the church and in 300 yards pass the Royal Arms Inn. In a further 100 yards turn left along a lane, with a high garden wall on the left. Pass the imposing entrance gates and notice the name of the dwelling. In 200 yards at the fork, turn right and in a further 100 yards turn left downhill. Follow this old road as it winds across the valley and up to the top of the hill opposite.

The first house you reach is Little Hall and in 200 yards there is a fine view over the valley to the wooded hills of Great and Little Doward. Continue to the entrance gates of Newton Lodge. Do not follow the lane round to the right but cross in front of the gates and keep next to the wall on the left. This leads to a narrow walled path, actually a part of the common, which soon widens out. Pass the cottage on the right and go straight over the track, to follow a path next to a hedge on the right. This soon becomes a hedged track, though the hedges are rather unusual. Five yards before reaching the lane, turn left in front of the houses and go along a grass track which runs parallel to the narrow lane. In 100 yards you emerge on to the open common next to the bus shelter, where the walk started.

Walk 23   Ross on Wye: Penyard Park

6 miles (9·5 km)

OS sheet 162

This walk starts from the town of Ross and goes over the hill which towers behind it. There are ample official parking places all round the town, which is not so large that a stranger will get lost, yet large enough to provide the amenities a modern community needs. This prosperous little town owes much of its character to its best known inhabitant who was born in 1637. He was John Kyrle, known locally as the 'Man of Ross'. Pope, in his *Moral Essays*, extols Kyrle's virtues with great feeling and without his usual satire, so he must have merited more than most men of his time. (Epistle III, lines 250–300). The church of St Mary stands high, overlooking the Wye valley. Go into the churchyard to start the walk.

From the row of attractive houses which line the north side of the churchyard, go to the left of the church to a small metal gate in the wall near a silver birch tree.

Keep straight ahead down a road, with first a clinic and then a police station on the left. Cross the main road (B4228) and bear left, to pass Dane Hill Hospital on the left. This road has an interesting collection of domestic architecture of all sizes, from the very old to the very new. Go down the hill until you come to a factory estate on the right. Here turn right and keep to the lane round the back of Associated Tyre Specialists. Walk along the lane for ¼ mile to Alton Court. That which is seen from the entrance gate is genuine 16th century, but the rear of the building, as seen from further back down the road, should not be looked at closely. Continue by going through a wicket gate at the end of the lane, signposted to Penyard. Follow the well-trodden path till it goes through a small metal gate into the bottom of a field. Immediately turn right and go up the field, keeping about 20 yards from the hedge on the right. As you start to go up you will see a sandstone fortress-like building coming into view, just to the left. As you climb higher you will become disillusioned. It is the front of a corrugated iron cover to a water tank. At the top of the field go over a stile which leads to a sunken track going off to the right. Follow the track until it comes out into a field. Here a number of paths meet. Turn left and go up the field to a stile into Penyard Wood. Beyond the stile go up the bank to a forest road and turn right.

Follow the forest road for ¼ mile. At the top of the rise look for a way-marking post on the left. A small track leads off from here to the left

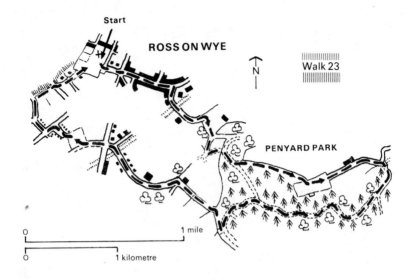

Start

ROSS ON WYE

↑
N
|

‖‖‖‖‖‖‖‖‖‖‖‖‖
Walk 23
‖‖‖‖‖‖‖‖‖‖‖‖‖

PENYARD PARK

0 _____ 1 mile

0 _____ 1 kilometre

between broom and gorse bushes. Above is a well-shaped, solitary and upstanding oak tree. Remember that the fruit of broom is very poisonous. In 10 yards look at the bank on the left, which is covered with an attractive lichen with the English name of 'Common cup'. To appreciate it properly you need a magnifying glass. If this lichen was ten times bigger than it is it would rank with flowers such as orchids. In 50 yards pass the gate on the left and follow the path at the edge of the wood, having the wire fence on the left. Look on the oaks on the right for galls. These are small round, pinkish-brown balls which the gall wasp, a small solitary waisted wasp, induces the oak to grow when it lays its egg at the base of a leaf. Inside the gall is a grub and later the grub makes its way to the surface and turns into an insect, leaving a neat round hole the size of a pin head to show where it emerged. At the bottom of the wood go over the stile on the right of the gate and into a field. On the other side of the field, where there are some large trees in the wood, is the site of Penyard Castle. Built in the 14th century, it belonged to the Talbot family but was in ruins by the 17th century.

Turn left along the field to a gate and on to the end of a lane. Walk along the lane past the farm on the left. In the wall of the barn, near the far end, you can see some pieces of carved stone. These must surely have come from the ruined castle. This is what happened to many of our ancient monuments, for they have so much of their building stone missing. The whole farm was probably built of free second-hand stone. Continue for a further $\frac{1}{4}$ mile and at the sharp left-hand bend, where the lane goes steeply downhill, turn right to a gate. Ignore the gate on the left. Go over the stile at the side of the gate and walk down the path. In $\frac{3}{4}$ mile fork right on to a forest road, which goes uphill. When it levels out and there are glimpses through the trees of distant wooded hills, look up in front. The tall oaks at the top of the wooded slope are those at Penyard Castle, which you saw from the other side. In $\frac{1}{2}$ mile pass a turn to the right and continue down the forest road. As you go down you pass a turn to the left and in 200 yards when you reach the bottom of the valley, look on the right for a wide opening in the trees. Here you can see the corners of two fields 50 yards away. Go down here towards a fence and turn right along a waymarked path, just inside the wood. Where there is a small clearing turn left to a stile, then turn right up into a field. Immediately turn left to a stile in the corner. Go over the stile and turn right uphill, keeping near to the fence on your right. Walk on up the sunken track ahead, past the entrance to the farm and so to the road junction. Cross straight over and go down the sunken road. After leaving the wood and passing the tidy factory on the right, continue down to the main road. Cross straight over, with care.

Follow the new road for 200 yards and go over a stile on the right. On the opposite side of the field, in the far left-hand corner, is a white house. It is at the left of this house that the footpath goes over a stile to the end of an old service road. Go down here to the main road and turn left. In 50 yards turn right along Cleeve Lane, which turns into a track and then forks. Bear right. When the track starts to go downhill, turn right up a flight of steps. Follow the path along the edge of two fields to another track. Turn right and in 20 yards, at the end of a wooden fence, turn left up some more steps. Notice the old gas lamp-post – alas, not working, and the two hinged arms on which the lamp man put his ladder. Continue along this path until it reaches the churchyard from which you started.

Walk 24

Ross on Wye: Brampton Abbotts

5½ miles (9 km)

OS sheet 162

Ross is the last town the river Wye passes before it enters the confines of the Forest of Dean. The town stands on the road from central England to the southern parts of Wales. It has always had the benefit of passing trade, with cattle and sheep going east or people going west. It is also an important local centre for farmers, as it still has a thriving cattle market.

The M50, a westerly spur of the M5, ends just outside the town. Travellers from the south have a choice of two routes, to go through Monmouth or Coleford.

There are many small car parks round the town and it is only a short walk from any of them to the churchyard, where the walk starts.

From the row of attractive houses which line the north side of the churchyard, go down the curved steps on the western side and turn right. At the main road through the town turn left. In 100 yards turn right and go down this road to the bottom of the hill, where it turns round to the right. In front is the cattle market and a short 'No Through Road'. Go up here, with the market on the left, to pass under a bridge. In a few yards fork right up a well-used footpath which climbs up the hill to come out on to a road. Turn left past modern Ross. At the top of the hill the road crosses over the dual carriageway of the link road connecting the M50 and the A40. From here you can see excellent exposures of old red sandstone on either side of the cutting. In a further 300 yards the road turns sharply to the right, but you keep straight ahead down a rough lane. This curves across the valley to the hamlet of Netherton. Here the farm on the left is also industrial, being the headquarters of the Netherton Farm Plan. Straight ahead is the corner of a field which has a farm gate with a kissing gate on its right. Go through here, up the bank and across the field to a second kissing gate. This type of gate was very popular in Georgian and Victorian England, as it formed a matching part of the iron railings round an estate. It enables people to get through but not animals. The gates were usually only three feet high, thus facilitating the more important function from which they derive their name. There are a number of these gates around Ross and most of them are in good order, having been renewed within recent years. Perhaps the demand for this design is greater here than in most parishes. Continue

80

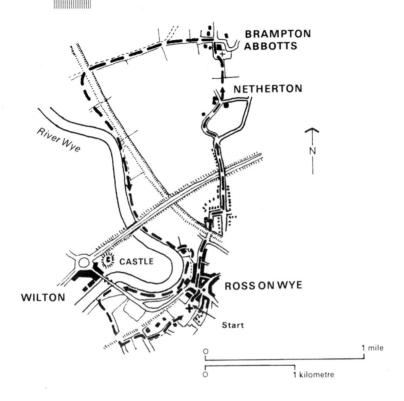

along the path, next to the fence on the right, into the churchyard at Brampton Abbotts.

Pass to the left of the church and then bear left into the corner of the churchyard. From here a narrow path goes past the School House to a small gate. Go through this gate and immediately turn left to follow the footpath sign. Keep to the left of the brick wall with attractive summer-house built into its corner and keep straight ahead with the hedge on the left. Go on down the hill for nearly $\frac{1}{2}$ mile to join a farm track. Keep the same direction along this track for another $\frac{1}{2}$ mile. At the old railway track the right-of-way goes to the left along two meadows just below the track to join a riverside path. The Tourist Board have a pleasant waymarked walk from the riverside path along the track to this point. Continue along the riverside.

81

In $\frac{1}{2}$ mile you go under the dual carriageway road that you went over on the way out. Walk on along the next meadow as far as the electricity pole and then bear left. This path goes round behind the boathouse, crossing two bridges, each with their gates. 'Disgusted of Tunbridge Wells' might well complain about the monolithic authority which, whilst adopting a traditional form of contrivance to regulate passage, can put spikes on top of a kissing gate! Continue through the park next to the river, passing the garden of the Hope and Anchor Inn on the left. In $\frac{3}{4}$ mile you can just see the remains of Wilton Castle, hidden in the trees, on the opposite side of the river. This is a genuine medieval castle, whereas that which graces the sandstone heights overlooking the river is an elaborate 1840 medievalisation. Pass under the end arch of Wilton bridge. This was built in 1597 and is fine example of 16th-century workmanship, with its massive cutwaters and ribbed arches. It has been skilfully widened to take motor traffic. In the centre of the parapet, there is an 18th-century sundial with the inscription:

Esteem thy precious time
Which pass so swift away
Prepare thee for eternity
And do not make delay

Continue along the riverside for 200 yards and then turn left over a stile. In five yards go over a second stile in front and then straight across the meadow. In 100 yards go to the right of the hedge to the far end where there is a stile. This leads to a path which turns into a track and goes up in a cutting in the sandstone cliffs. As you go up you come to two flights of steps, one on either side. This is part of Kyrle's Walk, named after the town's 18th-century benefactor. Turn left and climb the steps following the path to the next track in a cutting. Here turn right for 20 yards and then turn left again to follow the path to the churchyard.

As you go through the churchyard look over to the left where there is a Georgian arch. This was the south gate of The Prospect, a public garden which once occupied all the ground to the south, west and north of the church and is still a monument to Kyrle's generosity, though only a fraction of the original imaginative layout remains. It was because of this and his many charitable actions that he became known as 'The Man of Ross'.

Sellack is a tiny settlement three miles northwest of Ross on Wye. It is best reached from the Ross–Hereford road. From the roundabout at Wilton where the A449 (continuation from the M50) meets the A40 to Monmouth, go along the A49 Hereford road. Take the second turning on the right in ¼ mile, signposted to Hoarwithy. The turning to Sellack and Baysham is in two miles, which is half way between Hoarwithy and Ross. In a further ¾ mile turn left past Sellack school on a narrow lane down to the church and two houses.

The walk is along fields bordering the river Wye as it makes one of its great meanders.

The church of Sellack is dedicated to St Tysilo, a little known saint in England – but much of this side of the Wye is Welsh. ¼ mile further west from the church is Caradoc Court which is part stone and part timber, dating back to the 16th century.

The car can be parked on the grass verge near the churchyard wall. Keep well clear of the lane and gateways. The lane is used by farm vehicles which seem to get bigger and bigger each year.

Walk on round the churchyard wall. If the sun is shining and you want to know the time, the Georgian sundial on the tower can be read from the road but don't forget to allow for summer time if necessary. Pass the ruins on the left and at the end of the churchyard wall go over a stile next to a gate. From here you can see the next two stiles and the top of the metal footbridge. This magnificent footbridge is similar to one at Foy you cross on the way back. Could it have replaced a ferry? The houses you pass on the road ahead are in the parish of Kings Caple and form a small settlement marked on the map as Sellack Boat. Turn right at the road and in ½ mile, at the 'T' junction, turn right past the entrance to Poulstone Court. When the road makes a sharp bend to the left, leave it and go straight ahead, following the sign 'Public Bridleway'. Pass the cottage and go through a gate. Walk along the next field near the hedge on the left and go under the old railway bridge. Continue in the same direction past the stumps of elms which have been attacked by Dutch elm disease. Cross the stream by the stepping stones and go up the bank ahead, keeping near the fence on the left. Walk on along the top of the field past the remains of an old farmstead but all that is left is the yard which often fills with water.

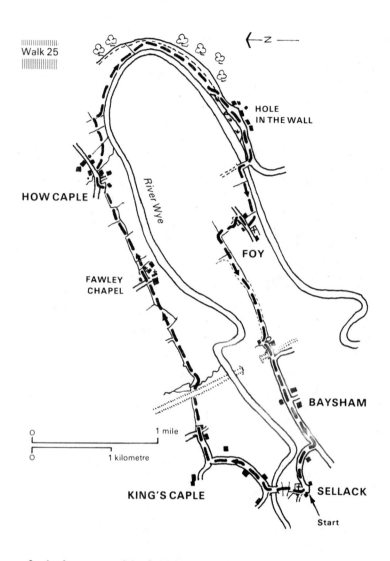

HOLE
IN THE WALL

HOW CAPLE

River Wye

FOY

FAWLEY
CHAPEL

BAYSHAM

1 mile

1 kilometre

KING'S CAPLE

SELLACK

Start

In the far corner of the field, by the well-shaped oak tree, go through a gate. From here the bridleway goes across the field to the far right-hand corner, where stand two oak trees. Aim a little to the right of the one on the left. Go through the gap in the hedge here and keep near the hedge on the left out to the lane at Fawley. As you go along, look over to the ridge on the right on the other side of the river – you will walk along the top of this on the way back. Fawley church is down the lane and then left. The court dates back to the 16th century and the house Much Fawley has 14th-century cruck trusses. This is almost all there is at Fawley.

Cross the lane and with the wall on the right pass the entrance to Seabournes. Go forward to a gate into the old farmyard. Walk on up into the field on the right and continue with the hedge on the left. Go through the gates with care as modernity is everywhere – after the string vest, the string hinge! $\frac{1}{2}$ mile past the farmyard there is an oak tree standing out in the field five yards from the hedge. Just past this go over a broken-down fence on the left of a gate. Behind it is a sunken track with a double hedge. This is part of the old road you have been following from Poulston Court to How Caple. Here for a short distance it can still be seen. As it is overgrown, go through into the field on the left and follow the hedge on the right down the hill. When the hedge ends there is a gate in front. Go through this and keep next to the fence on the left to a gate near a cottage. Here the bridlepath bears left across the field down to a road, not down the track ahead.

At the road turn right and in 100 yards turn right through a gate into a field. Walk across this field keeping about 20 yards from the hedge on the right. Go over two stiles and then straight ahead to a gate. In the next field to this gate the path divides. Turn right and with the fence on the right go to the stream and turn left. Continue along the edge of the field with first the stream and then the river on the right as far as the narrow grass field. Now follow the path along the side of the river or walk on the unfenced road a little higher up. In half a mile you come to Hole-in-the-wall, as you will see on the post box at the far end of the cottages. It is an old box as it has VR on it, even though it looks as good as new. Pass the River Wye Canoe Centre, opposite which are some islands which are fast turning into riverside meadows. Only at flood time are they again islands and in another 100 years the land will be almost level.

Walk on along to the footbridge and cross. At the other side turn left and walk along the riverside path to the beginning of the third field. On the right the church stands high with the old vicarage next to it. From this point they look as if they are joined together but they are actually quite far apart. Bear right to go up the middle of an old orchard with very few trees left, between the church and the large house on the right. This is Foy.

At the road the walk continues to the right. You may be interested in the church which has a 600-year-old door with hinges ornamented in the form of sickles. The churchyard has an interesting entrance. If you wish to see the church turn left but return and continue along the road.

In 200 yards, at the far end of the farm buildings, turn left into the farmyard and go across to the left-hand gate. Go through and walk next to the hedge on the right for 100 yards to a gate in front. Go through the gate and walk up this field with the hedge on the left. At the top of the field there is a small covered reservoir. You have to go over or round this to a gap in the end hedge. In the next field turn left and keep this direction along the top of the ridge for one mile. Fortunately in the second field there is a track to follow. There is a good view of Fawley to the right, where you were on the way out. Ross is to the left and the mountains of Wales in front. At the farm buildings go round to the right of the pond and continue along a stony roadway. The cottages on the left have a row of martins' nests under the eaves; these birds need to be house trained. Continue along a metalled road over the old railway bridge and at the lane keep straight ahead. In $\frac{1}{4}$ mile you go through Baysham! A little further on you come to the turning for Sellack. Turn right, pass the school and go down the hill to the church.

4½ miles (7 km)

OS sheet 149

The first part of this walk is along the side of the river and the return is through quiet trackways.

The village of Hoarwithy has many of its houses built on the steep hillside overlooking the river. The church, which dominates the village, was completed in 1890 and the 'scheme for decoration' was by George Fox who also worked at Longleat. The metal bridge over the Wye is quite modern, there being no bridge in 1803. At this time there were four ferries between Hereford and Ross but it is a shallow river with many fording places.

The village of Hoarwithy is three miles south of Hereford at an ancient crossing of the Wye. It is signposted on the A49(T) Hereford–Ross road and also on the B4224 Hereford–Mitcheldean road.

Cars can be parked at the river side of the road, ½ mile from the centre of the village, on the road to Carey and Bolston, opposite a wood on the hillside.

The walk starts from the corner of a large uneven field where there is a footpath sign, and goes to the riverbank. You will see a great ditch sweeping around to the left. This was once a part of the river and the footpath goes over what was once a group of islands. It was only in the middle of the last century that it began to dry out and the parish boundary still follows the ditch. Continue for one mile to the pillars of the old bridge which took the Hereford to Ross railway over the river. The railway was almost straight but, owing to the meanders of the river, it crossed the river three times in 2½ miles. At the stile just beyond the embankment, look across at the opposite hedge. Half way up to the left, it will be seen to turn sharp right for 50 yards, before continuing on up the slope. A hedged track used to end at this point. The footpath goes across the field and then along the track. If there is a standing crop you may find it preferable to go into the next field to reach the track but the right of way is across the first field. Follow the track up the hill to the lane and then turn left.

In 200 yards the lane goes over the railway track. There is the office block converted to cottages on one side and on the other side the goods yard, where the local farm produce was loaded for Hereford. Continue down the lane past Rock Farm into Carey. Do not turn left at the Cottage of Content but keep straight ahead, following the stream to

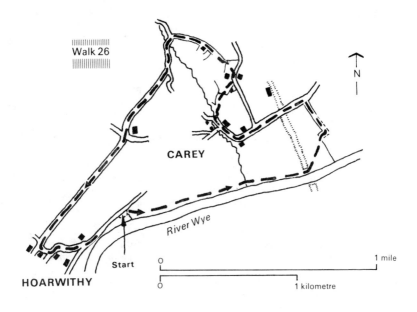

CAREY

River Wye

Start

HOARWITHY

| 0 | | 1 mile |
| 0 | | 1 kilometre |

the first sharp left-hand bend. Here turn right and cross the footbridge. Go up a flight of steps and then turn left to a gate. The path now winds along the bottom of a steep bank for 50 yards. Where it bears left, towards a grass field, go up the bank on the right. At the top of the bank, keep to the left of the field and go up to the top corner, winding round the bramble patches, to a stile. Bear slightly right in the next field, to a gate next to a white cottage and so on to the road.

Walk ahead up the road and in a few yards pass the first entrance to Carey Court on the right. A few yards further, opposite the second entrance, turn left over a fence into the corner of a paddock. Bear right and cross to the opposite corner and go through a wicket gate next to the field gate. In the next field there are fine views over the valley. Bear right along the top of the next field, next to the hedge on the right, to the corner. Continue along the start of a rough track, with an orchard on the left. This track improves as it goes downhill past the old buildings of Mountboon Farm. The old farmhouse has gone but the barns have been turned into a modern house, which is now called Barn House. Go down the track to the lane and turn left. In the bottom of the valley the lane goes over a stream. Until quite recently this was a ford. Many of the Herefordshire lanes had fords, in fact quite a lot still do, but motor cars and lorries do not like going through water – the horse and cart thought nothing of going through two feet of swirling stream. Continue up the hill and take the right fork. This used to be an important road but, as you will see, it soon becomes a hedged track, only fit for tractors. In $\frac{1}{2}$ mile, in the garden of the cottage called Point Pleasant, there is the framework of a reflecting telescope. The delicate parts are removed when not in use.

Cross the lane and keep with the track over the hill. As you go down the hill you can see the river below Hoarwithy. The church spire on the hill to the left is at Kings Caple. On reaching the lane turn left. Just past the derelict building on the right are the remains of a cider press in its original position. Follow the lane downhill to the road, turn left and keeping to the right-hand side of the road, return to the car.

2½ miles (4 km)

OS sheet 149

Brockhampton is a small hamlet six miles southeast of Hereford. It lies on the east side of the river Wye, well away from any main roads.

To reach it from the north and west, leave the B4224 road through Fownhope and turn along a lane past the church, signposted to Capler. Turn right at the first crossroads and continue for ¾ mile. From the south and east leave the A40 at the roundabout two miles from the end of M50 and go on the A49 towards Hereford. In ½ mile at the second turning on the right, go towards Hoarwithy and then bear right to cross the metal bridge over the Wye. In ½ mile turn left, signposted Brockhampton and continue for two miles.

Cars can be parked on the grass verge opposite the last but one house on the road towards Hoarwithy. If this is not possible, go on along the road towards Hoarwithy and draw to the side of the road, opposite an oak tree, 50 yards past the last house. Please keep well in near the hedge as farm vehicles, which seem to get bigger and bigger every year, use this road.

This is a very pleasant and easy walk.

Walk back along the road away from Hoarwithy. When you reach the wall of the school playground fork left, to go behind the school. This rough lane soon turns into a grass track between high hedges. After ¼ mile, pass a cottage on the right and notice the fine views down to the left. Continue to the lane and turn left.

In a few yards, opposite Capler Lodge, there is a small view-point constructed by the Brockhampton Court Estate. From the right-hand side of this small area you can see a track going up from the river through the wood. This is the route you will take at the end of the walk. Go on past the lodge and the wooden farm-type gates beyond. There is a path through here up to Capler Camp, one of the many prehistoric earthworks in the area. Unfortunately it is not possible to see very much of the camp as the right-of-way goes along a part of one side only.

Continue the walk down the hill, keeping to the right. Look over the edge on the left from time to time where there are some pleasant glimpses of the river far below. At the bottom of the hill turn left on to a track which comes back along the hillside below the road. This track goes down to the riverside and past a number of small quarries, now overgrown with trees. Were these in use when Hereford was being

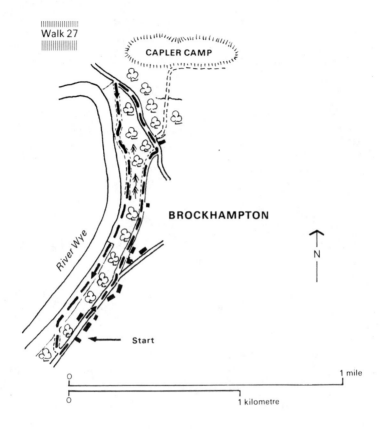

CAPLER CAMP

BROCKHAMPTON

River Wye

N

Start

| 0 | | 1 mile |

0   1 kilometre

built? They are convenient to the river and until the end of the 18th century most building stone was shipped by river wherever possible. It would be an easy journey upstream to the heart of Hereford. Pass the small hut on the left and walk on along the track through the trees.

On reaching a long narrow water-meadow, continue for $\frac{1}{4}$ mile to where there is a track going up the hillside, through the trees. At the bottom of this track, on the right, there is an old willow which has a split trunk and a number of its branches have cracked so that the tips rest on the ground. This is a good example of a crack willow. It is a summer flowering willow, as also is the white willow, from which it can be distinguished by not having white hairs on the underside of its leaves. The cricket bat willow is a hybrid of these two.

Walk up the track to the road and turn left back to the car.

Walk 28   Marcle Ridge Hill

6½ miles (10·5 km)

OS sheet 149

Marcle Hill is a long ridge seven miles east of Hereford and 1½ miles
west of Much Marcle. The walk starts from a lane which runs along
the ridge near a tall television relay mast. The countryside to the
north, west and south is a maze of small lanes, so it is best approached
from the A449 Ledbury–Ross road. From the crossroads at Much
Marcle (four miles from Ledbury and seven miles from Ross) take the
turning at the side of Westons Garage. This will take you past
Westons Cider and Perry Mill – so prominently advertised on the
sides of the garage. ¾ mile along this road, at the first crossroads, turn
right towards Woolhope. As you go up the hill the mast looms closer.
Near the top of the hill turn right and park on the grass verge, just past
the bend, leaving the gate clear for farm vehicles.

From the bend, walk with the mast on the right along the track which
goes over the hill. In 200 yards, at the highest point, Oldbury prehistoric camp can be seen just beyond the field on the left. It is one of
the earthworks which crown so many of the hills in these parts. Continue on the sunken track down the hill. In ½ mile you pass an old lime
kiln where the arched fire holes can be clearly seen. On the top, round
at the back, the small holes can still be seen where the limestone was
put in before firing to make lime for the fields and mortar for building.
After crossing the stream continue along a lane for 200 yards to the
top of the first rise and look on the right for a stile in the hedge. In the
field beyond, go straight across to the bottom corner and through a
gate. Now follow the hedge and stream on the right to a lane. Bear left
along the lane for 20 yards, passing the end of a barn, to turn right
through a gate. In this field turn left, gradually rising to the hedge and
fence on the right. In 100 yards go over a fence into the bottom corner
of another field. Go along the field, passing the orchard on the right.
Opposite the open barns, look for a fence on the left. The way out of
the field is over a stile in the far left-hand corner.

This is Sollers Hope. The early 16th-century black and white
farmhouse is on the site of the old manor house. By the end of the 16th
century the use of timber for building was declining, partly because of
its extravagant use in earlier years and partly because of the heavy
demand of the shipbuilders and ironsmelters. A house of this size
must have taken quite a number of fully grown trees. Behind the

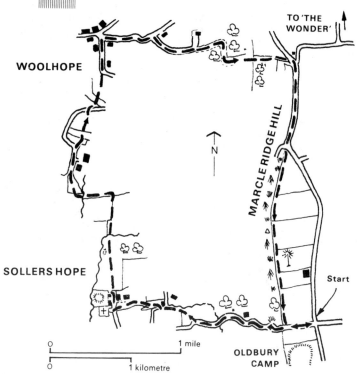

house and next to the church is a prehistoric tump and earth circle. In the early years of Christianity churches were built on top of these earthworks, thereby establishing the superiority of the new religion. Here, as at Kings Caple near the start of Walk 26, the church was built at the side of the sacred site.

Go through the farmyard with the house on the left, and in the field beyond follow the track. Do not fork left over the stream but continue along the field. When it narrows, with a wood on the right, go straight ahead to a fence. Keep in the same direction in the next field, with the hedge on the left. Continue for $\frac{1}{4}$ mile and go into the next field. Here turn left and go down to the corner where there is a new footbridge over the stream. In the field ahead there should be a stile in the hedge on the right and until it is replaced go on to the corner and enter the field on the right. At the far end of this narrow three-sided field there is a gate on to the end of a track. This track soon turns into a lane. Walk

93

up the lane and at the first left-hand bend go straight ahead through a gate. Follow the hedge on the right until it ends and then go forward to a gate in a fence. Now bear left across the field to a stile in the opposite hedge, 50 yards from the left-hand corner. From this stile go straight ahead, past the few remaining trees of an old orchard, to a stile on to the lane. Cross the lane and go over another stile. In the field turn right and go across the end of the field to a stile and footbridge. From the little footbridge bear slightly left to a stile in the hedge opposite. Go straight ahead from this stile, up the bank in front and then walk along the ridge to a gate and so on to a lane. Keep the same direction along the lane into Woolhope.

At the crossroads turn right down the hill on the road to Putley. In $\frac{1}{4}$ mile, just before reaching the car park of the Butchers Arms, turn right along a lane which winds up the hill. Keep ahead up the track, which eventually turns right along the hillside to a gate. Go through the gate and turn left up the hill next to the wood on the left. As you go you will notice, in the high bank on the left, how the layers of hard limestone, which form the hill, have been pushed up. This is the edge of Woolhope Dome, as described in Walk 30. Continue over the hill, past another lime kiln, to a gate in the hedge in front. From here follow the track down through the wood, keeping to the left just inside the wood. On leaving the wood go on to a gate and then down the edge of the field with the hedge on the left. In 100 yards pass through a wide gap in the hedge and continue with the hedge on the right. In the corner of the field, cross a track and go into the corner of the field in front. Walk on up the field with the hedge on the right. As you go up the hill you will see a sunken track the other side of the hedge. This is a continuation of the old road which started near the Butchers Arms. At the lane turn right.

In 1575 a great portion of the hillside near here slid gently down, burying a church and some houses. It has been known ever since as the Wonder Landslip. Should you wish to extend your walk and visit the site it will entail an extra $1\frac{1}{2}$ miles. To do so, go up the track at the side of the house opposite the gate you came through on to the road and in $\frac{1}{4}$ mile turn left along another track. This takes you to what looks like an old quarry but is where the slip started. It travelled downhill and a road goes over where it ended. Return to the lane.

Walk on up the lane and along the ridge. In $\frac{1}{2}$ mile, where the lane forks, a footpath goes on straight ahead. To reach the field in front go five yards into the old quarry and turn left up the bank. Keep along the top of the next three fields as far as the Ordnance Survey Column behind some windblown spindle bushes on the right. From here you can see across Herefordshire to the mountains of Wales to the west, to May Hill topped with a clump of trees to the south, and to the Malverns and the Cotswolds beyond to the east. Continue past the mast and in $\frac{1}{4}$ mile go down to a stile on to the sunken track you set out along at the beginning of the walk. Turn left back to the car.

This walk starts from Holme Lacy Church, which lies one mile southeast of the present village with only the old vicarage standing nearby. This isolated position, on the lowest ground in the parish, raises the question, Why here?

Perhaps Alfred Watkins can help. In 1920 this distinguished Herefordshire man realised that beacon hills, mounds, earthworks, moats and old churches built on pagan sites seemed to fall on straight lines. He did not interpret these mysterious lines, some of which stretched for many miles across the countryside, leaving later archaeologists, who are only now beginning to accept the evidence, to suggest an explanation. Holme Lacy Church lies on the intersection of two such lines, or leys as he called them. One ley which starts in Mid Wales goes through the churches of Belmont Abbey, Bullinghope, Holme Lacy, Fownhope and Sollers Hope and the edges of three prehistoric camps, all within a five mile stretch. The other ley aligns Aconbury Camp (a beacon) St Annes Well, Aconbury and Holme Lacy Churches, Mill Farm (a ford) and Woolhope Church, all within $3\frac{1}{2}$ miles. Such coincidences are well above the incidence of probability. Watkins in his book *The Old Straight Track* gives a number of examples from Herefordshire where minor evidence such as stones and moats have tended to survive longer than in other counties because the type of agriculture has not required their removal.

Holme Lacy is a small settlement four miles southeast of Hereford. It lies on the B4339 road which links the A49 in Hereford to the B4224 near Fownhope. Go along the road opposite the Agricultural College in Holme Lacy to Bolstone and the hospital. Pass the hospital entrance and in $\frac{1}{4}$ mile turn left, signposted Church Road. Go under the bridge and follow the lane down to the church.

Please leave clear the turning area in front of the church entrance and any gateways. There is sufficient parking space on the grass verge back along the lane towards the sharp bend.

Walk back along the lane to the sharp bend and keep straight ahead to a gate. In the field beyond, turn left and walk through the meadows by the side of the river. The trees growing in the bank are common alders. They like the moist situation on the river bank so that they can drink deep and despatch their children by water to a similar place downstream. Charcoal for gunpowder was made from Alder wood, so

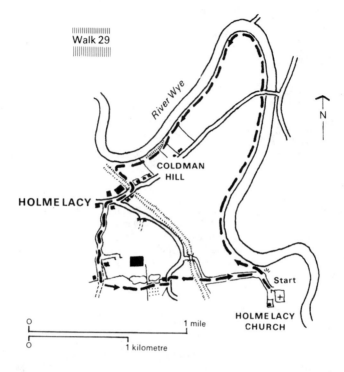

River Wye

COLDMAN HILL

HOLME LACY

N

Start

HOLME LACY CHURCH

0   1 mile

0   1 kilometre

many of the older trees have been coppiced and are now in bush form.

Continue past the road bridge for nearly $1\frac{1}{2}$ miles until you come to a hill. This is Coldman Hill. When you arrive at the top pass through a field with fine views down to the Wye on the right. Go on through rough ground at the back of a timber yard and into another field, taking care not to bear right down the hill. In 200 yards, at the first corner, the right-of-way goes on along the edge of the cliff down the hill. It then returns to arrive back into this field 100 yards to the left, in the second corner. Walk on by the side of the hedge which ends at the road, on the right of a white house. On reaching the road turn right and take great care as you cross the railway bridge, expecially at the far end, as there is no pavement.

Continue by the school of agriculture, with its well laid-out gardens, past Bower Farm. Just beyond the black and white house on the left, turn left. This is the rear entrance to Holme Lacy Hospital. Walk along this drive and when you come to a fork go right, round the corner of a high brick wall. Pass the extensive walled garden on the left and cross a cattle grid at the entrance to the park. A few yards past here turn left through a gate and bear right to go down the valley to the right of the lake.

96

As you go down you will notice a gigantic tree on the left. On measuring its trunk five feet from the ground, it was found to be just over 30 feet in circumference. A rough estimate for an oak tree, growing in the open, is that it starts at the rate of one inch in six months and at 360 inches would take four to five years to add a further inch to its girth. After some complex calculations it is suggested that this tree might have been a young sapling when Joan of Arc was burnt, some 550 years ago.

Holme Lacy House was built by the second Viscount Scudamore in the late 17th century and is the most magnificent setting for a hospital that could be imagined. With views of distant wooded hills across spacious lawns and lakes, it is the interior which is breathtaking. Stripped of all furniture and its best woodwork, it is still a thrilling experience to see the plaster ceilings, which are amongst the finest in the country. The first Lord Scudamore is today remembered for having propagated and made popular the famous cider apple called Redsteak. As a result Herefordshire has been the centre for British cidermaking for over three centuries, despite what they say in Devon and Somerset! During the 18th century tens of thousands of hogsheads of cider were made, some being exported to Bristol and London, where it was considered equal to any French wine. After the Napoleonic Wars there was a temporary decline in quality and quantity and it became the 'make-wage' for farm labourers. At the turn of the century, factories grew up in and around Hereford, three of which survive today – Bulmers, Symonds and Westons. There is a cider museum in Hereford which is worth a visit.

Walk on past the lakes to a gate into an orchard. Keep straight ahead along the bottom of the orchard and when the trees end go down to a gate on to the road beyond. Turn left along the road past the old school house and in a few yards go over a stile on the right. Cross the field, passing between the remains of an avenue of trees to the railway embankment. On the other side keep straight ahead along the lane back to the car.

Walk 30   Haugh Wood

3 miles (5 km)

OS sheet 149

Haugh (pronounced Hoff or Huff) Wood is four miles southeast of
Hereford. It lies on both sides of the road between Mordiford and
Woolhope, at about the halfway point.

Cars can be parked at the Forestry Commission car park at the
highest point in the wood.

There is a stone pillar on the left as you enter the car park. From
here you can purchase a leaflet which describes a most interesting
forest trail.

At the end of the Ordovician era (440 million years ago) the
Silurian limestones and shales were laid down at the bottom of
shallow seas. These were later folded and Devonian old red sandstone
(O.R.S.) laid down on top. Since then erosion has removed much of
the O.R.S. leaving the tops of the underlying folds exposed. These in
turn are now being weathered. Because the Silurian rocks are harder
they have worn away slower. This walk starts on the lowest layer, the
Cambrian sandstones (at least 500 million years old) and goes over a
number of different Silurian rocks. Walk 28 is entirely on Silurian
limestones and shales and Walk 20 is on the O.R.S. which forms most
of the Herefordshire plain.

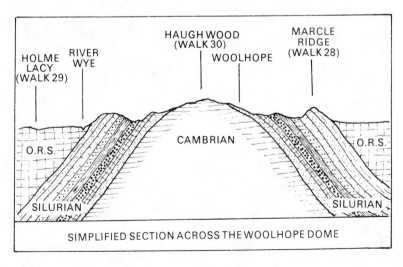

SIMPLIFIED SECTION ACROSS THE WOOLHOPE DOME

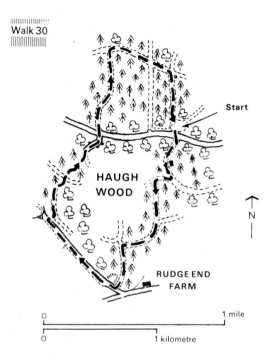

Start

HAUGH
WOOD

N

RUDGE END
FARM

0   1 mile

0   1 kilometre

Leave the car park by the main entrance, where you came in, and cross the road. Enter the wood by a forest road, follow it past the woodmen's huts on the left and in 100 yards bear left. In $\frac{1}{4}$ mile look on the right for a trail marker post. These are round posts about four feet high with, in this case, blue tops. They are put at all changes of direction on a trail. Here the trail comes towards you and turns down the grass track to your right. Follow this track and notice the great number of ants at work. Many ants have no sting but defend themselves by squirting formic acid at their attackers. Sometimes they can be seen carrying long slivers of wood ten times their own length. Think of carrying a floorboard 60 feet long, over rough ground – between your teeth!

Follow the track until you come to a fork. The trail goes up to the right, you go down to the left. When you come out on a forest road turn right. When this forest road sweeps up to the right to a wider and well-used forest road, turn left down the hill. As you go down you pass on the right the Rudge End Quarry Nature Reserve, managed by the Herefordshire and Radnorshire Nature Trust Ltd. These nature trusts are to be found in all counties. They do a fine job ensuring the survival of wildlife and preserving a balance between the needs of man for food production, recreation and housing. They also bring to the

99

notice of owners, users and planners of land the need for conservation, so that they do not unwittingly destroy what we need to conserve. Information about your local trust can be had from SPNC, The Green, Nettleham, Lincoln.

At the bottom of the wood go round the barrier and on to a 'T' junction with a good stone road. Turn right along the track which follows the bottom of the wood. To the left is typical Herefordshire countryside which has the remains of Victorian orchards and fields of eight to ten acres with smaller paddocks in between. The tops of the hills and the steeper sides are covered with oak woods. After $\frac{1}{2}$ mile you will see a gate in front of you. Stop five yards before reaching it and look on the right. Behind the nut bush on the edge of the track you will find a little gate into the wood. Go in here and in another five yards turn left up a rather overgrown forest track.

In $\frac{1}{4}$ mile, soon after the track levels out, there is a tractor track going up to the right. Follow this and in a few yards it turns left on to a forest road. Cross straight over to a narrow track through the trees. In 200 yards the path comes out on to a forest road. Keep ahead for 50 yards to a barrier. You are now at the end of a lane and as you go along you pass cottages. The lane leads out to a road. Bear left across the road to an entrance to the other part of the wood and a wide forest road. There are many smashed snail shells to be seen on this forest road. The snails live in the damp ditches and banks, mostly on the right. The birds find them but have to bring them out to where there is a hard surface before they can get at the snails inside the shells.

In $\frac{1}{4}$ mile, at the 'T' junction, turn right up the hill. Where the forest roads cross, go straight ahead. At the next crossing, where there is a black water tank on the corner, stop and look around. In front and to the left you can see the circle of wooded hills, a mile or so away. This is a ring of hard rocks round the edge of Woolhope Dome. You are standing on the dome now and the valley all round is slightly softer rock. Looking back over the track you came up you may be able to see Hereford.

Turn right along the hill-top. From time to time you get very good views to the right. Unfortunately, where the young trees have grown to about 15 feet the view disappears. The long flat hill in the distance is the start of the Brecon Beacons and the right-hand end is Hay Bluff. Continue to the car park.